HEARING-IMPAIRED CHILDREN
A Guide for Concerned Parents and Professionals

ABOUT THE AUTHOR

Mr. Bevan is a graduate of Gallaudet University, where he obtained a Master's degree in the education of the deaf, and of Hunter College, where he earned a Master's degree in audiology. In addition to teaching hearing-impaired children for several years, he taught graduate courses in the education of the deaf as an instructor at Pennsylvania State University and guest lecturer at Bloomsburg State College.

For nearly twenty years his administrative duties as Director, Child Study Department, at a large residential/day facility for the hearing-impaired has given him diverse and extensive experience with parents, staff, students and other professionals in the field.

Other experience as Chairman of the Communications Committee, Research Committee, Parent Education Committee, and Disciplinary Committee, as well as Director of Parents' Workshops, Diagnostic Clinics and Gallaudet Summer Learning Vacation, have added to his wealth of knowledge to compile the information set forth in this book.

HEARING-IMPAIRED CHILDREN
A Guide for Concerned Parents and Professionals

By

RICHARD C. BEVAN, M.S., M.A.

With a Foreword by
Robert Frisina, PH.D.
Vice President and Secretary of the Institute
Rochester Institute of Technology

C H A R L E S   C   T H O M A S   •   P U B L I S H E R
Springfield • Illinois • U.S.A.

Published and Distributed Throughout the World by

CHARLES C THOMAS • PUBLISHER
2600 South First Street
Springfield, Illinois 62717

© *1988 by* CHARLES C THOMAS • PUBLISHER

ISBN 0-398-05507-6

Library of Congress Catalog Card Number: 88-16009

Printed in the United States of America
SC-R-3

Library of Congress Cataloging-in-Publication Data

Bevan, Richard C.
    Hearing-impaired children.

    Bibliography: p.
    Includes index.
    1. Hearing impaired children — Rehabilitation.
2. Hearing disorders in children — Treatment.   I. Title.
HV2391.B48   1988   362.4'2'088054   88-16009
ISBN 0-398-05507-6

*To Jimmy and Tom, both of whom are
successfully overcoming their
handicap in spite of its severity.*

FOREWORD

Parents confronting hearing impairment for the first time are somewhat traumatized by the experience. Eventually, periods of despair, doubt, and self-searching can turn into boundless energy and support for a hearing-impaired son or daughter. And that is as it should be. Perhaps quite surprisingly, the challenge and commitment by parents that helps a child overcome serious obstacles to learning and adaptation to family and community can become a joy few others experience.

It has been said that the understanding of a problem contributes 50 percent of the solution. The author of this book aims to provide a solid foundation for better understanding of the challenge and potential unique to each child.

As you will discover, there is a good deal known about the medical, educational, psychological and sociologic aspects of hearing impairment. These known facts are described and illustrated throughout the book in an easy-to-understand way. Technical data are held to a minimum in order to help get you started in constructive ways that benefit both you and your child.

You will learn that ready development of speech and language are influenced by different degrees and types of hearing impairment. Application of hearing aids and specialized help in language and communication development are keys to early successes.

The author presents guidelines augmented by basic questions that parents should ask as their child moves from one stage of life to another. A goal of this book is to help parents become wise advocates on behalf of their children. Informed persistence on your part will assure best practices as your child undergoes his/her formal educational experience.

You will discover that the world holds out more hope and promise than you might have thought when first struck with the reality of a hearing-impaired child.

Experience suggests that successful hearing-impaired adults invariably have been blessed with parents who made the effort to become well-informed, who persisted in their efforts, and who instilled in their children attitudes of optimism with a willingness and drive to confront obstacles with confidence. Careful study of this book and the avenues of hearing it opens to you can be rewarding for you and your child.

ROBERT FRISINA

PREFACE

This book is designed for parents of hearing-impaired children, especially those who have recently learned about their child's hearing loss. If you fall into one of these categories and feel angry, alone, frustrated, or filled with despair, then the book's contents will help to alleviate some of these anxieties. For you are not alone. Other parents are experiencing the same feelings. With their help and that of professionals, you can assist your child immeasurably.

Although it is normal for you to undergo the various stages of the grieving process, the more quickly you accomplish this the sooner you can direct your energies toward constructive measures, thus effectively providing him with a stress-free environment. Grieving over your child's loss for a prolonged length of time will only delay your youngster's development. It is more important for you to reach a stage of questioning and understanding based upon the nature and implications of the handicap, as well as on what is available in the way of assistance. You will then be better prepared to act as an appropriate role model and become part of a support system for your child.

Successfully rearing any child requires a great deal of effort on the part of parents. The task becomes far more complex if a youngster is hampered by a handicap such as hearing impairment. Yet, if you arm yourself with sufficient information, exert the extra effort, learn more about the possibilities, and become more involved with your child's development, you will find that your participation will prove rewarding and indescribably satisfying.

When you read this book, your fears and your sense of hopelessness should begin to abate. It should also help you to plan for experiences that you would like your youngster to receive. Thus, your child should stand a far better chance of becoming an emotionally well-adjusted, productive, socially integrated individual—the goal of all loving parents.

ACKNOWLEDGMENTS

Through the many parents of hearing-impaired children that I have been privileged to know, my own life has been enriched and I have gained greater insight to present the information contained in this book. Without these experiences, this endeavor would otherwise have been impossible.

Special recognition is due to Dr. Kenneth Schrepfer, whose expertise, knowledge, and experience contributed heavily to the thoroughness and clarity of the material presented in Chapter 7, Psychological Evaluations.

Further acknowledgment is due to Dr. D. Robert Frisina, who reviewed the original manuscript and wrote the Foreword to this book.

Recognition is also due to Mrs. Emily Holmes and Albert Bochrach, who offered editorial comment throughout the writing of the manuscript.

I would also like to thank Lois Narzisi for her encouragement and exemplary attitude and management regarding the rearing of her own deaf child. In addition, I would like to acknowledge the support, excellent typing skills, and interest in this book by Estelle Sparks, whose encouragement not only stemmed from her recognition of the book's need, but was further intensified by her own long-standing hearing loss.

Special recognition is due to my wife, Frances, who added immeasurably to the book's contents through my exposure to her as an individual who has experienced a severe hearing impairment since early childhood. These experiences were further enriched by our mutual effort to assist with the rearing of a profoundly deaf child, Jimmy, a task that would have been impossible without her cooperation and less productive without her skills.

I would also like to acknowledge the many professionals, too numerous to name, whose contacts with me added immeasurably to my technical and practical experiences.

Without question, the book's clarity of content would have been greatly diminished without the talented artistic work of Sandy Cozzolino, whose familiarity with hearing-impaired children added to the clarity of the illustrations.

Finally, I would like to acknowledge the love and support of my parents, Warren and Ruth Bevan. without whom all that I have to offer would have been impossible.

CONTENTS

		Page
Foreward		vii
Preface		ix
Chapter		
1.	**The Grieving Process**	3
	Introduction	3
	The Grieving Process	3
	The Denial Stage	4
	The Bargaining Stage	4
	The Anger Stage	4
	The Guilt Stage	5
	The Acceptance Stage	5
	Summary	6
2.	**The Family**	7
	Introduction	7
	Family Description	7
	Acceptance by Parents	8
	Acceptance by Siblings	8
	Acceptance by Extended Family	9
	A Communication System	9
	Emotional Impact of Communication	10
	Social Impact of Communication	10
	Educational Impact of Communication	10
	Total Family Involvement in the Communication Process	10
	Behavior Management	11
	Educational Programming	12
	Out of School Activities	12
	Activities at Home	13
	Summary	13

3. **Anatomy and Physiology of the Ear**   15
    Introduction   15
    Anatomy   15
        Structure   15
    Physiology   17
        Function   17
        Air-conducted Sound   18
        Bone-conducted Sound   18
    Summary   21
4. **Etiology and Medical Treatment of Hearing Impairments**   23
    Introduction   23
    Conductive Causes and Their Treatment   24
        Congenital Malformation   24
        Cerumen (Wax)   24
        External Otitis (Outer Ear Infection)   24
        Otitis Media (Middle Ear Infection)   24
    Types of Otitis Media   25
        Nonsupperative   25
        Serous   26
        Mucous   26
    Other Conductive Causes   29
        Cholestatoma (False Tumor)   29
        Otosclerosis   30
    Sensorineural (Nerve) Losses   32
        Causes   32
            Congenital   33
            Acquired   33
        Treatment   33
    Mixed Type Losses   33
    Central Deafness   33
    Summary   34
5. **Audiological and Hearing Aid Evaluations**   35
    Introduction   35
    Audiological Considerations   36
    Subjective Tests   36
        Pure Tone Audiometry   36

Loudness 36
Frequency 37
Speech Audiometry 38
Types of Testing by Age 41
Testing Infants of 0–24 Months 41
Testing Children aged Two to Five Years 42
Testing Children Five to Eighteen Years of Age 45
Objective Tests 45
Impedance Audiometry 47
Tympanometry 47
Static Compliance 47
Acoustic Reflexes 47
Electrodermal Response Audiometry 47
Heart-Rate Response Audiometry 49
Electroencephalographic Evoked-Response Audiometry 49
Electrocochleography 49
Hearing Aid Evaluation 49
Summary 50
6. **Hearing Aids** 51
Introduction 51
Hearing Aid Components 51
Types of Hearing Aids 52
Hearing Aid Functions 54
Maximum Power Output 56
Gain 56
Frequency (Pitch Response) 56
Choice of a Hearing Aid 56
Which Ear 56
Dispensers 57
Character of Aid 57
Hearing Aid Performance 57
Summary 59
7. **Psychological Evaluations** 61
Purpose and Types of Tests Selected 61
Psychologists' Skills 62
The Setting 63

Intelligence Testing   64
Psychological Tests   66
    Hiskey-Nebraska Test of Learning Aptitude for
        Young Deaf Children   66
    The Leiter International Performance Scale   66
    Merrill-Palmer Scale of Mental Tests   68
    The Wechsler Tests   69
    The Stanford Binet Test of Intelligence   69
Developmental Evaluation   72
    House-Tree-Person and Human Figure Drawing   72
    Vineland Social Maturity Scale   73
    Parent Conference   73
Summary   74

8. **Language Development**   81
    Introduction   81
    Rules   81
    Developmental Sequence   82
    Considerations for the Hearing-Impaired   82
    Summary   84

9. **Speech and Hearing**   85
    Introduction   85
    Speech Characteristics   85
        Voiced and Unvoiced   85
        Placement of the Articulators   87
        Formants   88
        Speech Intensity   88
        Vocal Sound Following a Consonant   89
        Duration of Sound   91
        Absence or Presence of Sound   91
    Hearing Speech   91
    Speaking   92
    Summary   93

10. **Communication Systems**   95
    Introduction   95
    Pure Oral Method   96
    Fingerspelling (The Rochester Method)   97
    Siglish (Signed English)   97

Amslan (The American Sign Language) 98
Simultaneous Approach 99
Cued Speech 99
Total Communication 100
Summary 101
11. **Speech, Speechreading, Auditory Training and Manual Communication** 103
Introduction 103
Speech 104
Speechreading 105
Auditory Training 107
Manual Communication 108
Summary 110
12. **Legal Aspects** 113
Introduction 113
Rights to a Free Education 113
Assurances of Extensive Child Identification Procedures 114
Assurance of "Full Services," Goals and
    Detailed Timetable 114
Guarantee of Complete Due Process Procedures 114
Assurance of Regular Parent or Guardian Consultations 115
Assurance of Non-Discriminatory Testing
    and Evaluation 116
Guarantees of Policies and Procedures to Protect the
    Confidentiality of Data and Information 116
Assurance of Special Education in a Least Restrictive
    Environment 116
Maintenance of an I.E.P. (Individualized Educational
    Program) 117
Assurance for a Surrogate to Act for a Child
    When Necessary 117
In-Service Training 117
Architectural Barriers 118
Summary 118
13. **Educational Options** 119
Introduction 119
Programs 119

Total Mainstreaming 119
Mainstreaming With Supportive Services 120
Resource Room 120
Self-Contained Classes 120
Day Schools 120
Residential Schools 121
Home-Bound Instruction 121
Parent Role 121
Summary 122

14. **Individualized Educational Program Plan (I.E.P.)** ... 123
Introduction 123
Conferences 124
Pre-Planning Conference 124
Revision Conference 125
I.E.P. Contents 125
Present Educational Levels 125
Instructional Areas 127
Instructional Area 127
Annual Goal 127
Short-Term Objectives 127
Instructional Methods 127
Evaluation of Instructional Objectives 130
Summary 130

15. **Post-Secondary Education** 131
Introduction 131
Post-Secondary Education 132
Services Offered 134
Areas of Study 137
Summary 138

16. **Demographics** 141
Introduction 141
General Population 142
Etiology 143
Multiply Handicapped 144
Communication Systems 145
Speech Intelligibility 147

Academic Achievement 149

Summary 150

17. Devices for the Hearing Impaired 155

Introduction 155

Devices 155

Summary 155

Glossary 167

Bibliography 173

Index 179

HEARING-IMPAIRED CHILDREN
A Guide for Concerned Parents and Professionals

Chapter 1

THE GRIEVING PROCESS

INTRODUCTION

At one time or another, everyone suffers emotionally as the result of loss. This may be the loss of a family member, a friendship, or a bodily function. In each case, its permanence hurts: You have lost a part of yourself. If your child is suffering from a noncorrectable hearing impairment, the loss seems as permanent to you as the death of someone you love. Therefore, the grieving process is the same.

We are amazingly similar in terms of the sequential nature of our feelings. However, some individuals can pass through the various stages of grief more quickly than others. Then there are those who find themselves unable to bring the process to a successful conclusion, because their feelings have been locked at one particular stage. Others pass through several stages, then revert to a former one. Since the grieving process is an inevitable part of suffering from loss, it is important for you to understand its nature and the steps through which we need to pass to deal with it effectively.

Perhaps you have listened to a member of your family or a friend comment that you or your spouse have never fully accepted your child's handicap. This should alert you to the fact that one or both of you may still be going through an earlier stage of the grieving process. If your child's impairment has been established as permanent, only when you accept this reality will you be able to offer your youngster constructive assistance that will compensate for or overcome the handicap. Once you realize that there is hope for him to lead a successful, productive, happy life, you are likely to reach the acceptance stage. If his handicap is, say, partially accepted, you will not be able to offer him full assistance.

THE GRIEVING PROCESS

Since you are undoubtedly asking yourself just what the grieving process is, it might be wise to review the sequence of feelings that an individual experiences. Remember, you are not unique. Everyone, at some time, will have the same feelings. If you recognize this fact as perfectly normal, you will be better able to pass through its stages.

The Denial Stage

The first reaction to a physician's statement that your child is suffering from a noncorrectable nerve deafness is usually denial. The impact of the doctor's statement may be too much for you to face. Your bereavement is truly painful. You feel separated from your child because you wonder how you are going to communicate effectively, how he will talk, or how he will learn. You may feel that the physician and the audiologist who evaluated his hearing are unskilled, the testing was too brief, or the testing equipment was at fault. In short, you are in a state of disbelief and shock.

If you are honestly in doubt about the results of the evaluation, perhaps you should seek a second opinion. However, if you are doing so because you are denying the permanence of the hearing impairment, serious danger exists that you will drift from one physician or clinic to another, only to hear the same results. This will simply cause you unnecessary grief and expense. Worse yet, it will prevent you from dealing with your anxieties; for if you become fixed at this stage of the grieving process, you will be delaying necessary planning to meet your child's needs. This may cause him far more pain and suffering than you yourself are presently enduring. Your energies need to be diverted into more constructive channels, which will better enable the child to overcome the handicap.

The Bargaining Stage

It is typical of parents to think that it would relieve their youngster of pain and suffering if they themselves could assume the hearing loss. Often bargains are tendered. You may find yourself making promises to change your life for the better, or that you will purify yourself if what you have been told is not true. Sometimes you may fantasize, engage in rituals, or believe that somehow the hearing loss will magically disappear.

Bargaining is a way of keeping alive the hope that all will be well with the child.

The Anger Stage

Once you realize that your energies have been dissipated and your anxieties heightened through bargains that gave no results, you may become angry with yourself, your child, your mate, God, or whoever might have been instrumental in creating your feelings of despair. Although you may be slow to realize it, no one has intentionally planned to burden you or your youngster. Blaming yourself or others for creating the situation is futile and unproductive. Furthermore, it is emotionally draining.

If you keep in mind that isolation from your child need not be permanent, then you can stop blaming others for what you feel is your misfortune. There is hope in spite of the handicap. A host of methods and individuals stand ready to help him. You must become a key figure in the process, for you are his first and most intimate contact. Therefore, you yourself will be instrumental in setting the patterns for his success or failure.

The Guilt Stage

Eventually your anger will lead to a sense of guilt. You will begin to realize that you have been angry with innocent people. You, your child, your spouse, family members, friends, physicians, nurses, acquaintances have all hoped that you would have a perfectly normal child. Suddenly, you feel guilty that you have blamed others for a situation that is no one's fault. It is simply a fact that you may as well accept.

The Acceptance Stage

This is the final stage of the grieving process. Once you have accepted the fact that your child has a permanent hearing loss, you can begin to think and act with a clearer mind. You are now ready to weigh, judge, and evaluate the situation so that you can take the necessary steps to insure a measure of success. Fortunately, the handicap is not terminal, and much can be done to cope with it.

SUMMARY

Your child is patiently waiting for a helping hand, just as anyone with correctly functioning senses is, only your particular youngster will require added effort on your part. At times this will strain you both, mentally and physically. The rewards, however, can be far in excess of what you would have imagined. Although there may be times when you lose ground, dealing promptly with your emotions increases the child's chances for success.

Chapter 2

THE FAMILY

INTRODUCTION

If your doctor determines that your child's hearing can be improved medically or surgically, you may find that the hearing loss is only partial and may be restored. On the other hand, if evidence points to a permanent loss, you will need to take a different approach. The problem is one that you must manage; you yourself will be responsible for certain outcomes. Perhaps you may feel that this is disruptive to your life and that of the rest of the family; but you will be right only if you allow such thoughts to fill your mind. Your family unity need not be destroyed.

Can you lend your child a helping hand? Do you want him to be a fully participating member of the family? Can you insure that he or she will feel comfortable with you and others? Can you foster his enjoyment of a healthful home environment? Can you help him develop normal growth patterns? Can you offer him a feeling of security? Can you set the stage for his learning behavior?

You have no time for self-pity, for your youngster is patiently waiting. Decisions must be made. It is now, not later, that he needs your help. You and he can gain a great deal from the experience. If you meet the challenge, your family can make the difference between success or failure. Therefore, you should consider a few aspects that are important to the welfare of the entire family.

FAMILY DESCRIPTION

A family is considered a group of individuals related to one another and bound together. The nuclear family consists of a married couple and their children. The extended family includes relatives of the nuclear family and others who have been added through marriage or adoption. The family has the initial and most lasting impact on a child's early development: It provides the basic needs of life: food, clothing, shelter.

It is also the support system for social, emotional, and educational welfare. As the child grows older, more effort is spent interacting with the larger society. Much later, he will act independently. Finally, he is expected to achieve total self-sufficiency, usually by establishing another nuclear family.

Although your youngster is hearing-impaired, his needs are the same as they are for all children. The impairment should not determine the degree to which the family is able to provide these benefits. To ensure that your youngster is not denied a normal home life, certain measures should be taken.

ACCEPTANCE BY PARENTS

During the early years of life, along with complex genetic structures, the parents' words and deeds are largely responsible for their children's patterns of behavior. It is extremely important, therefore, that you assess the needs of your hearing-impaired youngster with emotions as free as possible of guilt, remorse, anger, or rejection. As indicated in the chapter entitled "The Grieving Process," considerable emphasis is placed upon the need for you to reach the acceptance stage as quickly as possible. Other children within the family, as well as extended family members, will respond according to your management of the situation. Through your knowledge, explanations, and example, they will be guided and helped. Through your initiative, your child can become a true member of his nuclear family.

Probably the most important need is for both of you to deal with your youngster in the same way. If you are at odds with one another as to who is to blame (one parent has accepted the handicap, and one has not, or future plans for your youngster differ widely), chances for full development will be diminished. Although much of this sounds as though it applied to any child, you should keep in mind that the issue is complicated by the hearing loss.

ACCEPTANCE BY SIBLINGS

It is not enough for you alone to deal with your hearing-impaired child. Brothers and sisters, if any, should also play an important role, for they must learn to understand why you are spending more time than usual with their brother or sister. Explanations and reinforcement of your love will be necessary; otherwise, jealousies will develop which could result in deep-seated resentments.

Your other children may feel that the handicapped one is a threat to their security, because of your divided attention and divided love. If the time that you devote to your handicapped youngster is unavoidably extended, there is a danger of even greater feelings of resentment. Remember, the effort that you expend on his or her behalf should not be at cross-purposes with your goal to maintain family unity.

ACCEPTANCE BY EXTENDED FAMILY

Your hearing-impaired child should be able to enjoy all family relationships. When extended-family members lack proper understanding of the situation, their actions often conflict with your efforts. If you are trying to create an environment that allows your youngster to blend with the family, you will not want some members behaving in ways opposed to your wishes. Therefore, all your accumulated knowledge should be shared with them, and they should be made aware of the nature of the child's impairment, the extent to which it is handicapping, your attitudes regarding the management of the problem, and your expectations.

Keep in mind that many family members do not know how to react. They expect you to set the pattern. What you and your youngster do not need is pity, for that would only set him apart from family activities. Engage in honest discussion, demonstrate your goals, and make an effort to enlist their aid.

A COMMUNICATION SYSTEM

The choice and use of an effective communication system should be made as early as possible and enforced by all members of the family, because your child's need to communicate is the same as that of any youngster with normal hearing. In fact, it is the basis for social, emotional, and educational growth. Without it, he or she would be partially or entirely isolated, and this would have serious consequences, for he would then not only find difficulty functioning within the family but would also be faced with an even larger problem when confronted by the general community.

EMOTIONAL IMPACT OF COMMUNICATION

If your child is unable to understand daily verbal communication within the family, he will feel lonely and insecure. Later on, feelings of guilt may develop, eventually leading to a sense of inferiority. His desire to be a part of the family clearly exists, so if you fail to accommodate to the handicap, he may not try to learn to do so, and emotional problems far more complicated than the hearing loss will result.

SOCIAL IMPACT OF COMMUNICATION

Let us assume that there are no activities from which your child wants to be excluded. If the activity is one in which he is unable to participate, he should be included in the verbal communication involved. Common sense, although not very common, will dictate which activities he can manage, and as a general rule he should be included in the verbal communication connected with the activity on every occasion.

EDUCATIONAL IMPACT OF COMMUNICATION

By the time the average normally hearing youngster enters school, a vocabulary of five to seven thousand words has been developed, and the structure of the language is nearly intact. In effect, the family has been the teacher, and the home the classroom; therefore, your task is to duplicate this situation in so far as it is possible with your handicapped child. This alone should greatly assist you with the selection of a communications system, as noted later in this book. Ask yourself which will provide him with the opportunity to acquire and express language in a rapid, accurate, easily understood fashion. Once you have chosen which one is best, what he learns at home will develop foundation skills for formal classroom activity provided by the school of your selection.

TOTAL FAMILY INVOLVEMENT IN THE COMMUNICATION PROCESS

Your child is in need of immediate communication. You and the other children living in the household are his main contacts. These are the individuals who can provide the greatest amount of language. The willingness of all members of the family to use the selected communications system is critical; thus, consistency cannot be sufficiently stressed. If only one member of the family uses the method, your child will tend to turn only to that person for understanding. This is undesirable because he will place too much dependence upon that individual, and considerable language exposure that could be provided by other members of the family will be lost.

Usually, mothers more quickly accept their child's impairment. Communication seems to take on more urgency. Since the mother maintains closer contact with an infant, she will devise ways in which she can relate more easily. As a result, she is more apt to accept the handicap and instinctively want to help her child cope with it. Fathers tend to fantasize about their children's future, long before they are born. Therefore, they are less apt to accept the handicap. It is easier to occupy themselves with activities about the home that allow them to avoid the problem; while, during the day, they can preoccupy themselves with their employment. This does not, however, relieve them of their responsibilities, nor does it provide the child with proper exposure to language. You will need to resolve these issues through frank discussions although it is recognized that every parent really wanted a perfect child.

Children are usually more adaptable because they do not feel threatened by the impairment, especially if it is not visible. They are more ready to accept and do what is necessary to accommodate. Given proper direction, other children in the family can prove to be your youngster's most valuable resource. If there is closeness in age levels, your hearing-impaired child will engage in frequent activities with them. Knowing that a special means of communication is needed, they will learn to use the method chosen more quickly than most. Their contribution should not be underestimated.

BEHAVIOR MANAGEMENT

Once you have determined the communication needs, your child deserves no further advantages that are not enjoyed by your other children. If he or she understands and is able to express thoughts in an intelligible manner, further allowances for the hearing loss are less than beneficial. Provided you have established a pattern of behavior management for your other children, there is no reason why your hearing-impaired child should not be dealt with in a similar manner. If communication is clear, continue to treat all of your children the same. Often parents and educators think or say, "But the child is hearing-impaired." This is pity and does not provide a service.

If you overcompensate, the child will learn to use the impairment to manipulate you. Probably nothing is more harmful to family unity than overprotection of one member. The ground that you should be willing to give is an understanding of your child's needs and a reasonable certainty that you and other family members are communicating effectively. Your child will deal with the rest, much like any other youngster.

Although your interest in your child is important, there is no need for you to be overly conscientious. Do not be so determined to create happiness that it nearly kills you. It is normal for anyone to experience periods of frustration. Happiness is not an end in itself; it is a by-product of living. Your child needs room to mature, not just to grow. You cannot do all of this for him, since experience is usually the best teacher.

EDUCATIONAL PROGRAMMING

Your hearing-impaired youngster's education will require considerable preplanning. Although you may wish to modify the program from time to time, you should make certain that the method of communication you use and that of the child's school are the same. Activities conducted in the classroom may often be transferred to the home where a great deal of reinforcement can take place. You must therefore keep in close contact with the teacher, especially during the early grades where most attention will be given to language development.

Many states or counties offer nursery programs for hearing-impaired children between birth and five years of age. If one is available, take advantage of it. Remember, your child's lack of communication has created a language problem that is not easily resolved. Since he has much to gain from language exposure, it is never too early to begin such programs to enhance the development of better skills.

OUT-OF-SCHOOL ACTIVITIES

If your child is enrolled in a residential program for the hearing-impaired, extracurricular activities may be provided by the school. Although many are not available through local educational programs, especially during the early grades, perhaps you will find that they have been organized separately within the community. You should seek out these programs in which your child can participate and offer information as to his communication skills in order that the activity involved may prove beneficial.

Unless multiple handicaps exist, you should assume that engagement in these activities is healthful. It will allow your child to function independently of you. These experiences are needed to develop maturity and to learn what the real world is like. Your goal is to foster communication skills and confidence as well as minimize the handicap.

ACTIVITIES AT HOME

If you have considered how you will modify your communication system, the rest is just good judgment. Whenever your child can and should be included in the activity, allow it. Obviously, if it is beyond his age level, active participation cannot be expected, but remember that any conversation surrounding these activities should be made known to your hearing-impaired child. Normally hearing children enjoy this exposure. At first, this may seem strange to you if you are using any method other than a purely oral one. Nevertheless, keep in mind that every language experience is valuable. You have changed the communication system to meet your child's needs, not yours. Your goal is to allow him or her to become a part of the everyday family activities.

SUMMARY

The family serves as the most important part of your hearing-impaired child's growth and development. It is critical, therefore, that you accept the handicap, select an appropriate communication system, and take steps to provide your child with a normal, healthy home environment. You will set the stage for all that follows. At times this may seem a difficult task, but the rewards will be well worth the effort. If you approach the problem with confidence, you will find that issues which seemed unsurmountable will resolve themselves.

Chapter 3

ANATOMY (STRUCTURE) AND PHYSIOLOGY (FUNCTION) OF THE EAR

INTRODUCTION

As you have been advised that your child is suffering from a hearing loss, you will want to know whether or not it can be medically treated or surgically corrected. In many instances, your physician will advise you that the defect can be partially or completely eliminated. On the other hand, you may be told that the loss is of a permanent nature. In that case, a host of questions will enter your mind, for example: What caused the defect? Is the loss of hearing correctable through the use of a hearing aid? How great is the loss? Shall I be able to communicate with him or her? Will he learn how to speak? How will he learn?

To understand what you have been told about your child's hearing impairment, you should know the basic parts of the ear and how they operate. The following sections describe the structure of the ear and how each part functions.

ANATOMY

Structure

The ear is divided into three major parts. They include the Outer, Middle, and Inner Ear. The Outer Ear is made up of an external shell-like structure (Pinna) and the ear canal (External Auditory Meatus). The Middle Ear includes the eardrum (Tympanic Membrane), a cavity filled with air just beyond the eardrum (Otic Cavity), three small bones located within the cavity (Ossicles), and a tube that extends from the back of the throat to the Middle Ear (Eustachian Tube). The Inner Ear consists of a snail-like structure (Cochlea) which houses fluids and approximately 25,000 nerve endings (Cilia) that, on leaving the Inner Ear structure, join like the strands of a rope (VIII Cranial Nerve), to enter the center of hearing in the brain. Also included in the Inner Ear are three canals (Semicircular Canals) that are connected with and contain the same fluids as the snail-like structure that houses the nerve endings of hearing (See Figs. 3.1 & 3.2).

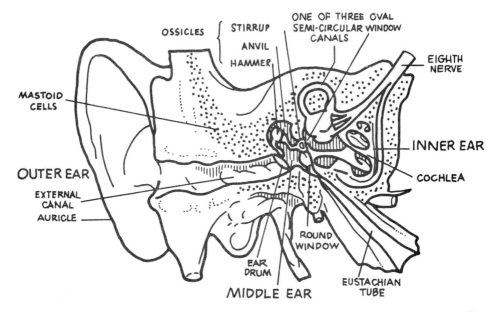

Figure 3.1. Sectional diagram of the human ear showing the Outer, Middle, and Inner Ear.

The Outer Ear is designed to collect the sound and transmit it to the eardrum. The Middle Ear bones transmit the sound from the eardrum to a small window that enters the Inner Ear. The tube that connects the back of the throat with the Middle Ear is designed to permit air to enter the Middle Ear cavity, resulting in equal air pressure on both sides of the eardrum. This allows the drum to move freely so that it will respond to sound properly. Once the sound enters the Inner Ear, the nerve endings are activated, permitting messages to ascend to the brain where they are interpreted. The three interconnected canals of the Inner Ear help us to maintain our balance and orient us in space (See Fig. 3.3).

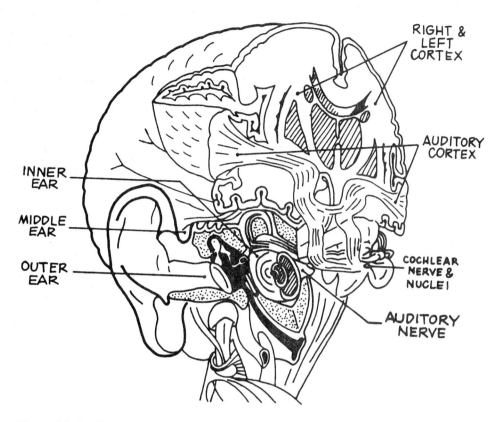

Figure 3.2. Sectional diagram of the ear as to position in the skull, parts of the ear and the pathways leading to the brain.

PHYSIOLOGY

Function

To gain a clearer understanding of your child's defect, you must know how sounds are normally conducted from their source to an individual's brain. In your child's case, some part of this chain has been obstructed, causing an interruption of sound. The causes of these blockages and which ones can be medically or surgically treated will be covered in another chapter entitled Etiology.

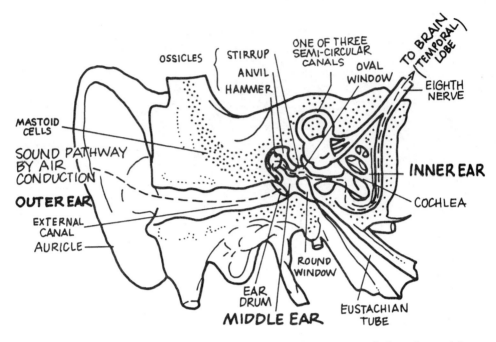

Figure 3.3. Sectional diagram of the human ear showing the transmission of sound from Outer to Inner Ear mechanism.

Air-conducted Sound

When someone speaks or environmental sounds are made, they pass through the air in a wavelike motion. Once they reach the human ear, they are collected by the Outer Ear structure, passing through the canal of the ear as "airborne sound." In turn, sound activates the eardrum, setting the Middle Ear bones in motion. During this stage, it is referred to as "mechanical energy." After crossing this chain of tissue and bone structure, sound passes through a window into the Inner Ear which is filled with fluids. During this stage, it is referred to as "hydraulic energy." When sounds activate the hairlike fibers of the Inner Ear, they are changed to electrical impulses which are caried to the brain by a bundle of nerves. The brain accepts these electrical impulses and interprets the sounds, which is where understanding actually takes place (See Fig. 3.4).

Bone-conducted Sound

In addition to airborne sound, we can also hear by bone conduction, since the Inner Ear is surrounded by bone (mastoid). Through vibra-

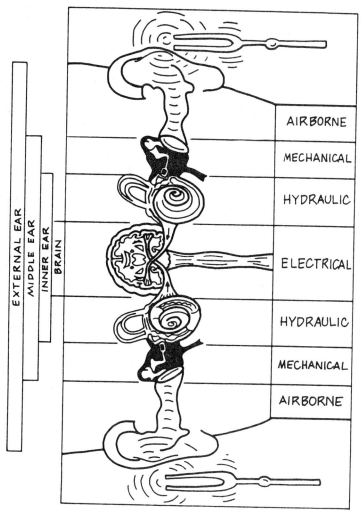

Figure 3.4. Sectional diagram of the human ear indicating type of sound transmission from the Outer Ear to auditory centers in the brain.

tions of the skull, sounds are able to bypass the Outer and Middle Ear structures, directly entering the walls of the snail-shaped Inner Ear. The sound activates the fluids of the Inner Ear and is converted to electrical impulses when it is sensed by its nerve fibers. These impulses are, in turn, transported to the brain center where they are interpreted.

Unfortunately, this form of transmission is less efficient than air-conducted sound, but it is still used when certain types of hearing loss are present. Because of the thickness and density of skull bones, sound must be made considerably louder to reach the Inner Ear. When it crosses the bones of the Middle Ear, it tends to be retarded in the process. However, this action is helped by the shape of the eardrum and movement of the Middle Ear bones, which actually increases the loudness of softer sounds traveling through bone structure. The skull, which is far more rigid, has nothing to compensate for the lack of efficiency created by bone-conducted sound.

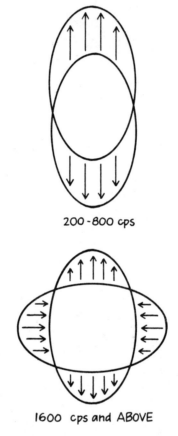

Figure 3.5. Movement of the skull bones as a function of frequencies generated by speech or environmental sounds that are a combination of a wide frequency band. Reproduced from *The Measurement of Hearing,* Ira Hirsh, with permission of the publisher, McGraw-Hill Book Company, 1221 Avenue of the Americas, New York, N.Y. 10020. Copyright ©1952. Rights reserved.

If the nerve fibers of the Inner Ear are operating properly, sound conducted through the skull bone is heard the same as by air conduction. It needs only to be made louder to obtain the same results. However, higher pitched sounds, which provide the most understanding of speech, generate the least amount of intensity. Unless they are made much louder, they will not be sensed by the nerve endings of the Inner Ear so easily as they are when they are introduced by the air-conduction channel.

An example of this lack of balance is demonstrated by normally hearing individuals using their own voices. Although they are hearing their speech by air and bone conduction at the same time, the air-conduction channel is more efficient; therefore, the sounds of their speech are received by the nerve fibers of the Inner Ear at a greater loudness level than by those same sounds conducted through bone conduction. Because their loudness by bone conduction is not strong enough to vibrate the skull bones, some of the sounds are being conducted by air conduction only (See Fig. 3.5).

SUMMARY

To fully understand the extent and nature of your child's hearing loss, it is important for you to grasp a knowledge of the ear's parts and how they function. If your youngster has suffered from nerve-type damage located in the Inner Ear, amplification, in the form of a hearing aid, will most likely be required. Should you find that the loss is due to a defect in the Outer or Middle Ear, surgery or medication may correct the problem. This will be discussed more fully in the next chapter entitled "Etiology and Medical Treatment."

Chapter 4

ETIOLOGY AND MEDICAL TREATMENT OF HEARING IMPAIRMENTS

INTRODUCTION

As parents of a hearing-impaired child, you need to know something about the various causes of hearing loss, what parts of the hearing mechanism are affected, and what can or cannot be done to correct these defects.

There are three basic types of hearing loss. Conductive types are those that cause improper functioning of the Outer and Middle Ear. Sensorineural ones are those that affect the Inner Ear mechanism, especially its nerve endings. Mixed-type losses are those that partially affect the Outer and Middle Ear, also resulting in some damage to the nerve endings of the Inner Ear.

Your physician should advise you where the defect is located, what can be done to correct it, how this will be accomplished, and what the possible results may be. If medical and surgical procedures are not indicated, he will recommend hearing aids. You will probably be referred to a hospital clinic, or an audiologist for an appropriate recommendation.

Should your child's loss be of a mixed nature, perhaps the conductive portion may be corrected through medication or surgery. Although you may be advised that the hearing loss cannot be eliminated, you should be on the alert to detect any causes of further damage. Observe your child's listening behavior, watch for signs that he is experiencing ear discomfort, and arrange for regular visits to your physician's office for ear examinations.

CONDUCTIVE CAUSES AND THEIR TREATMENT

Congenital Malformation

This is an absence or malformation of the Outer Ear shell, often accompanied by damage to the canal, Middle Ear parts, or possibly the Inner Ear structure. In many cases this damage can be repaired. If the hearing cannot be fully restored, your youngster might be fitted with a hearing aid that will allow sound conduction through the skull bone. If the Outer Ear is reconstructed, it is frequently possible to use an air-conduction instrument.

Cerumen (Wax)

If an excessive amount of wax accumulates in the ear canal, it may be impacted, preventing airborne sounds from reaching the eardrum. How rapidly it will accumulate depends upon the individual. Take your doctor's advice, since some wax in the canal is normal. Never, in any way, attempt to remove it yourself. You may damage the walls of the ear canal or cause impacted wax.

Wax should be removed by the doctor, who will flush or withdraw it from the canal. If it fills the canal and hardens, drops often will be inserted to soften it. Sometimes it can be removed immediately; or, if it has hardened, drops may be left in for several days before its removal.

External Otitis (Outer Ear Infection)

Sometimes changes in the skin tissue of the ear canal will permit the growth of bacteria or fungi, causing inflammation or infection of the canal walls. These abnormalities will usually respond favorably to medication applied directly to the walls of the canal and shell-like structure of the Outer Ear.

Otitis Media (Middle Ear Infection)

This is an inflammation or infection of the Middle Ear cavity, caused by any number of infectious diseases or allergies. Usually, these are upper respiratory infections transmitted through the tube leading from the back of the throat to the Middle Ear cavity. Such diseases can cause inflammation of the Middle Ear cavity, eardrum, Eustachian tube, and mastoid bone, often causing a reduction of oxygen supply to the cavity, or fluids to develop in the Middle Ear (See Fig. 4.1).

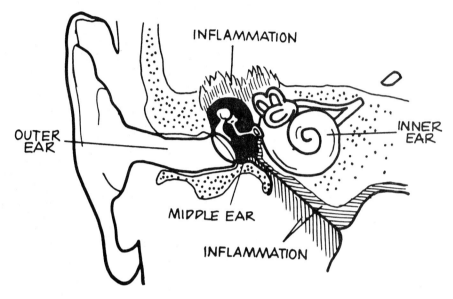

Figure 4.1. Diagram of the Middle Ear showing areas of inflammation as the result of diseases or allergies.

TYPES OF OTITIS MEDIA

Nonsupperative

The infection may cause inflammation of the tube leading from the back of the throat to the Middle Ear cavity. If the tube closes because of this inflammation and the Middle Ear fails to receive a continuous supply of oxygen, the air pressure outside the eardrum becomes greater than that of the Middle Ear cavity. The eardrum will then stretch inward, preventing it from properly responding to airborne sound (See Figs. 4.2 and 4.3).

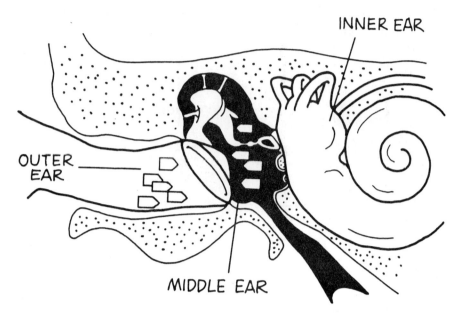

Figure 4.2. Diagram of healthy ear showing normal air flow and pressure at both sides of the eardrum.

Serous

A thin fluid develops in the Middle Ear cavity, pushing the eardrum outward and preventing airborne sound from passing through the eardrum and Middle Ear bones efficiently. If the fluid fills the Middle Ear cavity, it may shatter the eardrum and cause permanent damage. This form of Otitis Media is often referred to as a common cold in the Middle Ear. It is usually the direct result of an upper respiratory infection which passes through the tube leading from the back of the throat to the Middle Ear (See Fig. 4.4).

Mucous

Fluid thickens in the Middle Ear cavity, adhering to the eardrum and Middle Ear bones. This is usually caused by serious Otitis Media left untreated, or it may be of a chronic nature, often referred to as "glue ear."

Otitis Media is more common among children because the tube leading from the back of the throat to the Middle Ear is straighter and shorter, making it easier for infections to pass into the Middle Ear cavity.

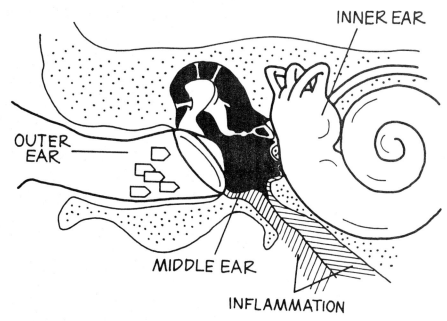

Figure 4.3. Diagram showing inflammation of Eustachian Tube as a result of disease or infection causing greater air pressure at the outer side of the eardrum.

As the head structure lengthens with age, the tube grows longer and lies at more of an angle.

If the problem is of a nonsupperative type, the physician will only make a tiny incision in the eardrum, equalizing the air pressure on both sides. Once the Eustachian tube is clear of infection, the incision will usually seal itself. Often, this condition will respond favorably to antibiotics; but, should the Eustachian tube be completely closed, requiring the eardrum to be punctured, it is called a "myringotomy." (See Fig. 4.5).

If fluids develop in the Middle Ear, the physician will make the incision in the eardrum larger. In addition, a small tube will be inserted to allow for better drainage. Usually the tube is rejected in two to eight months. Occasionally, it is necessary to remove the tube and patch the incision so that the tissue of the eardrum grows together more quickly. Once the infection is cleared, hearing will return to normal, or near normal. If fluids are left in the Middle Ear cavity, pressure on the eardrums may result in a perforation or shattering of the eardrum (See Fig. 4.6).

Your physician will always recommend that you purchase ear plugs if the eardrum has been punctured or a myringotomy has been performed.

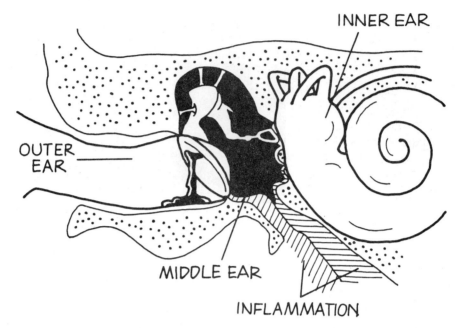

INNER EAR

OUTER
EAR

MIDDLE EAR

INFLAMMATION

Figure 4.4. Diagram showing basic parts of the ear, pressure of fluid build-up in the Middle Ear cavity and the shattering of the eardrum to relieve this pressure.

Although you can buy these plugs ready-made, it is better to obtain them customized since they will then be more snugly fitting. Without a tight seal, they are virtually useless.

You should, if possible, avoid eardrum punctures or perforations, for three reasons:

(1.) Drainage could be a continuing problem.
(2.) Tissue may grow into the Middle Ear cavity, sometimes developing into a dangerous false tumor.
(3.) If the infection is left unchecked and the eardrum bursts, scar tissue may develop, or a permanent hole may remain in the eardrum.

Because any of these reasons could result in permanent damage to the ear, you should be alert to the following symptoms which indicate a Middle Ear infection: (1) drainage of fluid from the ear; (2) complaints of an earache; (3) changes of hearing.

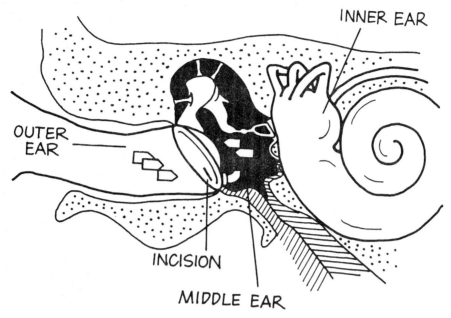

Figure 4.5. Diagram showing a surgical incision of the eardrum to relieve pressure created by fluid build-up in the Middle Ear cavity.

OTHER CONDUCTIVE CAUSES

Cholesteatoma (False Tumor)

If fluid continues to drain from the Middle Ear and remains untreated, then tissue may grow in the Middle Ear cavity causing a false tumor. Unless surgically removed, the tumor can continue to grow, shatter the Middle Ear bones, and invade the Mastoid bone surrounding the ear. Worse yet, it may invade the Meningis, the membrane covering the brain, and eventually cause brain damage.

Although a Cholesteatoma can be removed surgically, in extreme cases it may be necessary to remove part or all of the Middle Ear bones, the eardrum, and the infected cells of the Mastoid bone. (Surgery is almost always necessary.)

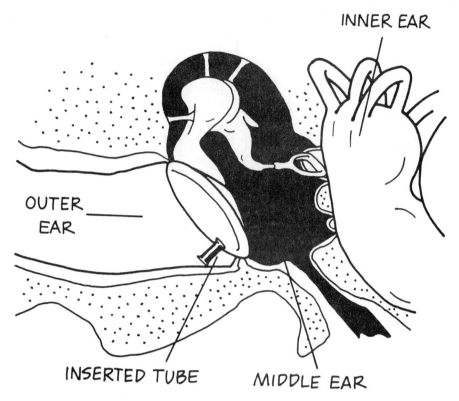

Figure 4.6. Diagram showing the basic parts of the human ear with a small tube placed at the incision to allow for better drainage of Middle Ear fluids.

Otosclerosis

The Middle Ear bones are named after objects that they resemble. The bone nearest the eardrum is the hammer (Malleus), the middle bone is the anvil (Incus), and the one closest to the Inner Ear is the stirrup (Stapes). Sound is normally conducted from the eardrum across these three bones to the oval window, which is the entrance to the Inner Ear. When a spongy bonelike growth develops around the Middle Ear bones, they are unable to move freely and sound cannot be transported across them to the Inner Ear. This growth is referred to as Otosclerosis (Oto: ear; sclerosis: hardening.)

This disease can cause as much as half of an individual's hearing to be affected when sound is conducted through the air channel. But, except in more advanced cases, the nerves of the Inner Ear are left intact; therefore, speech sufficiently loud can be heard normally.

Surgically, this type of hearing loss can be corrected through a stapedectomy (Stape: Stapes bone; -dectomy: surgically removed).

The Stapes is the most susceptible to the spongy bonelike growth, especially between the stirrup and the oval window. During the operation, the eardrum is set aside so that there is easy access to the Middle Ear bones. The Stapes bone is removed. Then a small wire is looped around the Incus. On the other end of the wire, body tissue is inserted over the oval window membrane. Finally, the eardrum is replaced in its original position. This procedure restores the conductive chain, and the improvement of hearing is excellent provided there is no nerve damage to the Inner Ear (See Figs. 4.7 and 4.8).

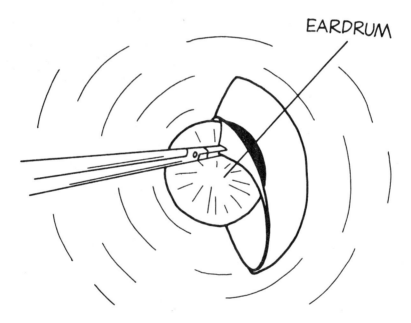

EARDRUM

Figure 4.7. Diagram showing the setting aside of the eardrum for access to the Middle Ear bones.

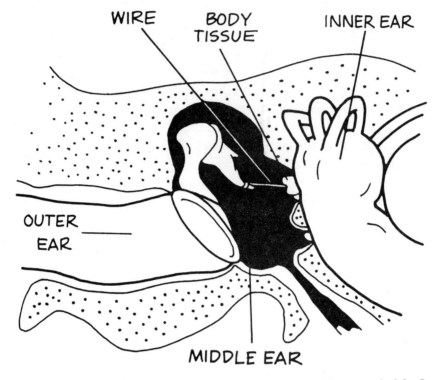

Figure 4.8. Diagram showing insertion of wire and body tissue after removal of the Stapes.

SENSORINEURAL (NERVE) LOSSES

CAUSES

Nerve-type damage to the hearing mechanism is present when the Outer and Middle Ears are functioning normally, but the nerve fibers located in the Inner Ear are partially or fully damaged, preventing sounds from being properly changed to electrical impulses. The understanding of speech will be affected, depending upon the number of hair cells damaged. If only a few have been affected, amplification will provide excellent understanding; but if the damage is extensive, understanding will be greatly reduced.

Congenital (Pre-birth)

1. hereditary
2. damage during pregnancy
3. causes unknown

Acquired

1. disease
2. injury
3. drugs
4. aging
5. exposure to loud sounds

Treatment

Nerve-type losses can often be arrested. Once damage has taken place, however, the nerve fibers of the Inner Ear cannot be restored. The only possible correction is through a hearing aid. If the cause of the potential loss can be eliminated before the nerve damage takes place, it can be arrested.

MIXED-TYPE LOSSES

These types of hearing impairment indicate that part of the hearing loss is caused by an obstruction or disease of the Outer and Middle Ear mechanisms, whereas part of the loss is due to nerve damage: perhaps a combination of any of those listed under Conductive and Nerve losses (pp. 24–32). To correct the conductive portion of the impairment may be possible, but nerve damage cannot be repaired. Decisions must be left to the surgeon, who may wish to perform an operation immediately, delay it for several years, or not perform it at all.

CENTRAL DEAFNESS

Any interference of sound transmission between the brain stem and the cerebral cortex is referred to as "central auditory disorders." The cause may be:

1. a tumor
2. abscesses
3. vascular changes in the brain

4. brain damage resulting from a trauma
5. blood incompatability

Central deafness is a neurological disorder quite different from the hearing losses already described. If deafness was acquired prior to the development of language, it is often difficult to demonstrate that it is different from a nerve loss.

Correction of central deafness goes beyond the skills of an ear, nose, and throat specialist, falling more appropriately in the area of neurology. It is not correctable through the use of surgery or medication.

SUMMARY

Hearing losses are of three basic types: conductive, sensorineural, mixed. If the loss is conductive or of a mixed type, there is a strong likelihood that it can be corrected by surgery or medication. Sensorineural impairments cannot be corrected, other than through the use of a hearing aid. Depending upon your child's degree of hearing loss, the benefits of an aid may range from perfect clarity to an awareness of sound. As you will find in subsequent chapters, some benefit can be derived regardless. You should not, therefore, assume that there is no hope for your youngster because the loss of hearing has been diagnosed as nerve damage.

Chapter 5

AUDIOLOGICAL AND HEARING AID EVALUATIONS

INTRODUCTION

Once an otological evaluation is completed, an additional examination may be indicated. An audiologist, a specialist in evaluating hearing, will not only determine the presence of a hearing loss and the degree and nature of the impairment, but he will assist with your child's rehabilitation. If surgery or medication can correct the loss, the otologist will proceed accordingly. On the other hand, a hearing aid evaluation will be scheduled if your child has nerve damage.

Once the hearing aid(s) have been obtained, the audiologist will decide whether or not they are operating properly, whether or not the settings are adjusted to give the most benefit, and how well the user is performing with the instruments. The audiologist should also offer you assistance with the instrument's care and maintenance and advise you regarding its expected performance.

Be cautious about accepting advice from your doctor or clinical audiologist regarding your child's educational program. Your district Director of Special Education or Director of Speech and Hearing is better prepared. He will be assisted by educators of the hearing-impaired, a psychologist, and frequently an audiologist employed by the county to service school-age children. As a team, these people are better prepared to initiate an appropriate educational program.

To understand the nature and extent of your child's hearing impairment as well as the benefits of amplification, you should know what factors to consider when the extent and type of hearing loss are measured. In addition, you should understand how a hearing aid is selected. The accuracy of the selection and of the aid itself are both important to your child's success with the development of speech and language.

AUDIOLOGICAL CONSIDERATIONS

The equipment and types of tests that an audiologist will use depend upon the child's age. At any rate, testing should be conducted in a sound-treated booth so that outside noises can be eliminated and the loudness of sounds introduced through earphones or loudspeakers can be controlled. Based upon your youngster's age level and the tests selected for use, it may be necessary for two individuals to evaluate his or her responses. You may be asked to take part in these procedures. Obtaining accurate measurements of hearing during the first two years of a child's life is difficult, so every resource must be considered. These estimates need to be made as early as possible, so that profit from any remaining hearing can be realized.

SUBJECTIVE TESTS

Pure Tone Audiometry

Most of the information that an audiologist gathers can be charted or recorded on an audiogram. This is a hearing profile that describes how your child compares with persons who have normal hearing. Much of the information can be obtained from you because you have been observing your youngster's listening behavior since birth, a fact that can be extremely valuable to the audiologist, who may be relating to your child for the first time. The audiogram will show the nature and degree of the hearing loss as well as the loudness level required for comfortable hearing and understanding. The degree of accuracy will depend upon the patient's age, when the hearing impairment occurred, the amount of hearing loss, the extent of language development, his or her attention span, and whether or not other handicaps are involved.

There are several factors that your audiologist will consider. Although they may appear to be quite complicated, you can grasp the fundamentals without undue effort.

Loudness

Loudness is measured in decibels, but it is not necessary for you to understand how this scale was devised. What you should know is how it relates to a person with normal hearing. The zero point through 20 decibels is considered within normal limits. As you move down the scale, sounds must be made louder. The average loudness level for conversational speech is 55 to 60 decibels. Therefore, if there is evidence of a 60 to 70 decibel loss, most speech sounds will fall below the range of hearing. Various degrees of loss are described by category, based on the measured decibel loss (See Figs. 5.1 and 5.2).

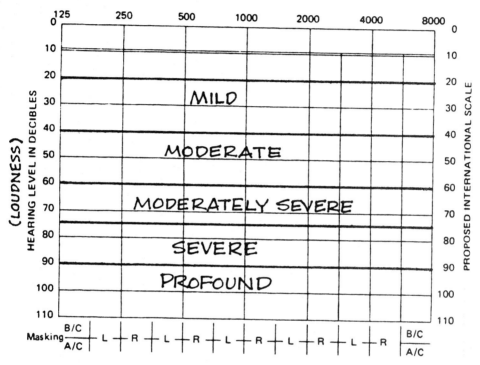

Figure 5.1. Based on the decibel scale, the various degrees of hearing loss are shown.

Frequency (Pitch)

By measuring the degree of hearing loss at various frequencies from low to high tones, it can be determined whether your child is able to hear speech delivered at a normal loudness level, at which level these sounds are being heard, and approximately which ones are understood. Testing the degree of hearing loss at various pitches, however, varies with age. Newborn infants require sounds to be intense before they elicit a visible response, which makes it difficult to obtain an audiogram that reflects the degree of hearing loss across the entire pitch range. Once a child is able to pay attention to the sounds and respond in a fashion that can be readily observed, the measurements of thresholds (the least loudness level at which sounds can be heard) are more accurate (See Fig. 5.3).

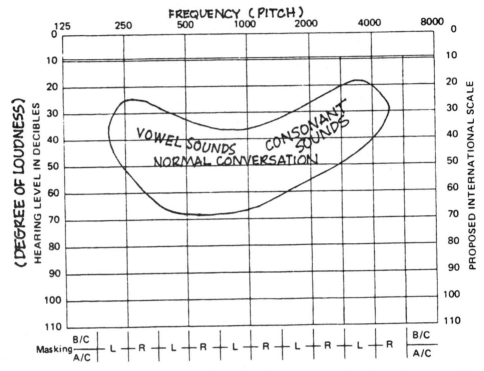

Figure 5.2. Area of speech sounds as a function of frequency and loudness when speech is given at a normal intensity level.

Speech Audiometry

When an audiologist tests your child using speech, several methods are available. Although it may be possible to obtain only an awareness level, he will want to know at what loudness the child can barely hear and understand speech. This is referred to as a "Speech Reception Threshold" (SRT). It is obtained by using two-syllable words, as shown in the following list:

Children's Spondee List

1.	sidewalk	20.	sunset	39.	hopscotch
2.	birthday	21.	daylight	40.	jumprope
3.	cupcake	22.	footstool	41.	shoelace
4.	airplane	23.	pancake	42.	hairbrush
5.	headlight	24.	hotdog	43.	necktie
6.	blackboard	25.	outside	44.	ashtray

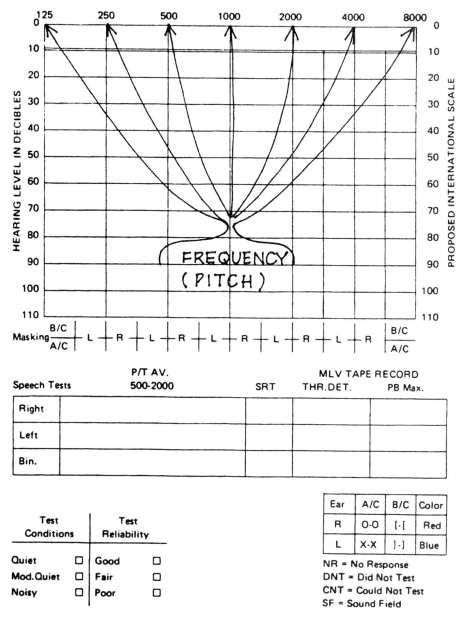

Figure 5.3. The various frequencies tested to determine the degree of hearing loss incurred from low to higher pitches.

7.	shotgun	26.	scarecrow	45.	bedroom
8.	eyebrow	27.	playmate	46.	toy shop
9.	railroad	28.	rainbow	47.	playpen
10.	baseball	29.	toothbrush	48.	dollhouse
11.	stairway	30.	dishpan	49.	highchair
12.	armchair	31.	bathtub	50.	downtown
13.	playground	32.	jacknife	51.	meatball
14.	doorstep	33.	ice cream	52.	sunshine
15.	mousetrap	34.	schoolroom	53.	barnyard
16.	cowboy	35.	backyard	54.	bus stop
17.	wigwam	36.	doorbell	55.	football
18.	coughdrop	37.	drugstore	56.	bluejay
19.	churchbell	38.	streetcar	57.	birdnest

It is also important to determine how much your child understands when speech is delivered at a comfortable loudness level. This measurement is called a "speech discrimination test," which is a list of words that contain the various sounds of the English language and the frequency with which they appear in ordinary conversation. Language limitations, degree of hearing loss, and the audiologist's ability to gain a child's confidence will determine the accuracy of these measurements. Such lists are referred to as "Phonetically Balanced Kindergarten" (PBK) lists. They have been devised on the basis of normally hearing children, so they assume that age level and exposure to language are similar. If your child has never heard speech and has limited language skills, this type of testing is unproductive.

Kindergarten PB Word Lists

List 1

1.	please	14.	rag	27.	bath	40.	neck
2.	great	15.	put	28.	slip	41.	beef
3.	sled	16.	fed	29.	ride	42.	few
4.	pants	17.	fold	30.	end	43.	use
5.	rat	18.	hunt	31.	pink	44.	did
6.	bad	19.	no	32.	thank	45.	hit
7.	pinch	20.	box	33.	take	46.	pond
8.	such	21.	are	34.	cart	47.	hot

9.	bus	22.	teach	35.	scab	48.	own
10.	need	23.	slice	36.	lay	49.	bead
11.	ways	24.	is	37.	class	50.	shop
12.	five	25.	tree	38.	me		
13.	mouth	26.	smile	39.	dish		

List 2

1.	laugh	14.	turn	27.	feed	40.	as
2.	falls	15.	grab	28.	next	41.	grew
3.	paste	16.	rose	29.	wreck	42.	knee
4.	plow	17.	lip	30.	waste	43.	fresh
5.	page	18.	bee	31.	crab	44.	tray
6.	weed	19.	bet	32.	peg	45.	cat
7.	gray	20.	his	33.	freeze	46.	on
8.	park	21.	sing	34.	race	47.	camp
9.	wait	22.	all	35.	bud	48.	find
10.	fat	23.	bless	36.	darn	49.	yes
11.	ax	24.	suit	37.	fair	50.	loud
12.	cage	25.	splash	38.	sack		
13.	knife	26.	path	39.	got		

TYPES OF TESTING BY AGE

Testing Infants of 0–24 Months

The response that the audiologist is seeking from this age level is an indication of sound awareness. From 0–13 months, responses range from sleep arousal to eye blink, shifting the eyes toward the sound source, startle reflex, and locating the sound by turning the head. During the early months of life, loudness must be at intense levels.

The most effective sounds at this age are produced by a variety of noisemakers, such as a bell, a rattle, a rubber squeeze toy, or Cellophane, to mention but a few. Although these items cover a fairly wide pitch range, they are louder at certain tones. The noisemaker can be held close to a child's ear, or it can be introduced through loudspeakers, which will allow more accurate control of the loudness level. Although these methods are not so precise as other tests administered at older ages, they are excellent screening devices.

Between 13 and 24 months, simple statements can be added to the testing procedures. The child need not understand them, since turning the head toward the sound source is sufficient. During the latter months of this age range, he may be able to respond to commands or questions.

Testing Children Aged Two to Five Years

Although children will differ in terms of attention span, ability to understand directions, and degree of hearing loss, it is usually possible to condition youngsters of this age using play audiometry. The technique requires putting a peg in a board when the noise is heard. If your child is nonverbal, conditioned responses may be difficult, and so the audiologist will have to rely upon awareness responses. If your youngster is verbal, the audiologist may ask him to repeat the words or ask that he point to objects or pictures representing the words. Sometimes, a judgment must be made as to whether a child has the necessary vocabulary to respond correctly. In any case, the tests give a fairly close estimate of the child's threshold of hearing.

Next comes a measurement of thresholds, using pitches or tones. To determine the location of the hearing loss, the latter should be introduced through earphones, then through a bone oscillator placed behind the Outer Ear. Testing by air and bone conduction will determine whether the hearing loss is nerve damage or the blockage is located in the Outer or Middle Ear. Such findings can be amazingly accurate.

Figure 5.4 shows the record of a youngster three and one half years of age conditioned with play audiometry. Responses indicate nerve damage of a moderate to moderately severe level in both ears. That it was nerve loss was determined because there was no difference between measurements by air or bone-conducted sound, indicating that all the loss was in the Inner Ear. Speech audiometry is in close agreement with the various pitches. Because of limited language skills, it was not possible to determine how well speech was understood.

This child was seen at a later date for a hearing aid evaluation and fitted with two behind-the-ear hearing aids.

Figure 5.5 shows the record of a verbal child with a moderate hearing loss. The measurements by bone conduction are normal, leaving a gap between the air and bone conduction results. Because this child demonstrated excellent receptive and expressive language skills, she was given a list of words to determine how well she could understand speech. The

AUDIOLOGICAL RECORD

Name _____ JOHN _____   Audiometers _____
Age _____ 3.5 YEARS _____   A/C _____
Date _____ 11/28/86 _____   B/C _____
Tested By _____   Speech _____

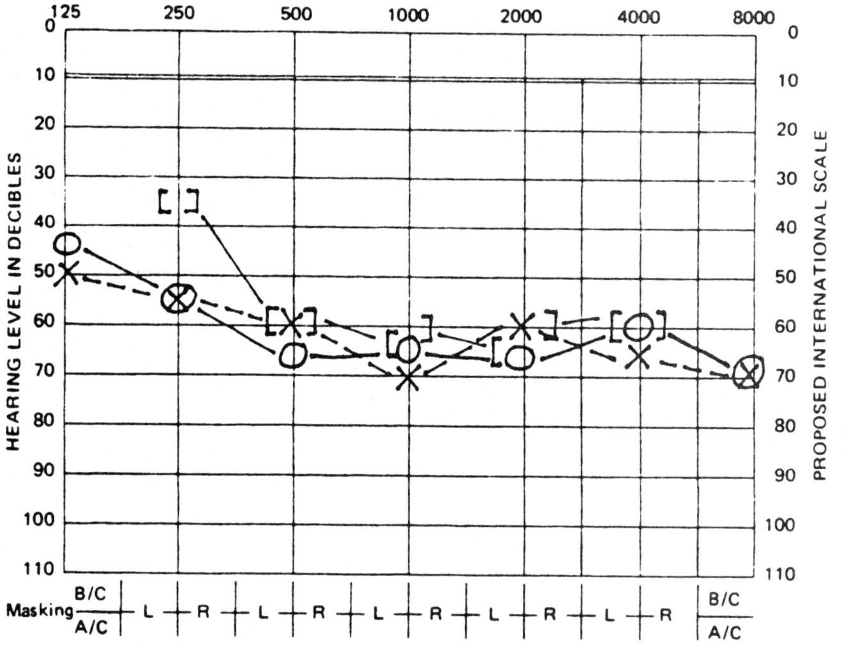

Speech Tests	P/T AV. 500-2000	SRT	MLV TAPE RECORD THR.DET.	PB Max.
Right			65	CNT
Left	66	65	60	CNT
Bin.				

Test Conditions		Test Reliability	
Quiet	☑	Good	☑
Mod.Quiet	☐	Fair	☐
Noisy	☐	Poor	☐

Ear	A/C	B/C	Color
R	O-O	[-[	Red
L	X-X	]-]	Blue

NR = No Response
DNT = Did Not Test
CNT = Could Not Test
SF = Sound Field

Figure 5.4. Audiological test results showing a 3.5-year-old child with a moderate to moderately severe sensorineural hearing loss.

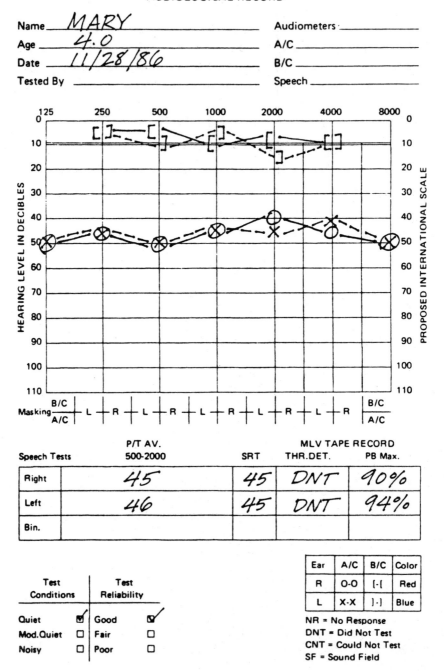

Figure 5.5. Audiological test results of a 4.0-year-old child with a moderate conductive hearing impairment.

test was administered using a series of plates, each containing pictures of four objects. One of the objects corresponded to the word presented, and the child was required to point to the correct picture. The results of these tests indicated that the youngster had some type of obstruction in the Outer or Middle Ear. When her Outer and Middle Ear were bypassed, she responded to sound at normal levels, and when speech was made sufficiently loud, her understanding was excellent because the nerve endings of the Inner Ear were intact.

Results confirmed the physician's examination, which indicated that the child had fluid filling the Middle Ear cavity. The eardrum was therefore punctured, and a drainage tube inserted. Eventually her hearing was restored to normal.

Figure 5.6 shows a youngster with a profound loss of hearing in both ears, indicating uncorrectable nerve damage. The parents reported that she used no understandable speech and failed to respond to any sounds. Testing was limited to tone responses and an awareness for speech in both ears. The child was recalled for a hearing aid evaluation and fitted with two powerful behind-the-ear hearing aids.

Testing Children Five to Eighteen Years of Age

At five years, most children can be tested like an adult. Unless mental retardation, brain damage, or over-activity exists, they can be trained to respond to sound at or near threshold levels. If they have been receiving and expressing language before the testing procedures, lists of words can be used to determine a threshold for the understanding of speech, and separate lists used to determine the degree of speech understood when it is made sufficiently loud. Care must be taken that the child understands what is expected and whether or not sufficient language skills have developed. Otherwise, the test is of language, not of hearing.

OBJECTIVE TESTS

A number of objective tests can be administered that require no response. Problems, if they arise, are usually associated with the child's inability to sit quietly while the test is being administered. In some instances, sedatives may be given. The instrumentation used provides certain involuntary responses, since bodily functions, over which the child has no control, are measured. An example of this is the administra-

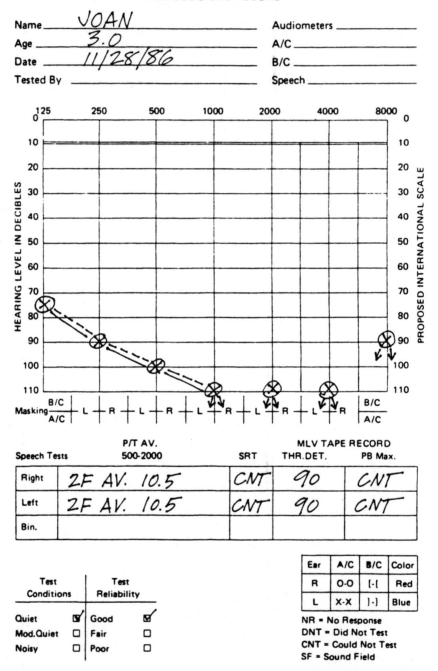

Figure 5.6. Audiological test results of a 3.0-year-old child with a severe to profound sensorineural hearing loss.

tion of a lie-detector test, in which case verbal responses are required, while the polygraph measures changes in body function.

Impedance Audiometry

This type of audiometry provides information supportive of standard audiometric techniques and includes a determination of the following:

1. the existing Middle-Ear air pressure
2. how mobile the eardrum is
3. how the Eustachian tube is functioning
4. how the muscles of the Middle Ear are functioning
5. whether or not the individual is responding appropriately through other methods of testing

This testing includes three types:

1. **Tympanometry.** By varying the air pressure in the ear canal, at what point it is equal to the pressure inside the Middle Ear cavity can be ascertained. This gives evidence of the presence of fluid in the Middle Ear, whether or not the Eustachian tube is functioning normally or whether or not a mass, such as a Cholesteatoma, is partially filling the Middle Ear.

2. **Static Compliance.** This test reveals whether or not the Middle Ear bones are moving properly so that sound can be transmitted to the Inner Ear mechanism. In other words, the springiness of these bones must be established. If they are stiff, they will retard the passage of sound, and responses will be absent at high-intensity levels.

3. **Acoustic Reflex Thresholds.** This test discloses how well the stapedius (stirrup) muscle functions. Its purpose is to retard sounds too loud for the human ear, which is designed to slow the action of the stapes. If there is no response at maximum intensity levels, the muscle is not reacting properly.

Tympanograms are classified into types as shown in Figure 5.7.

Electrodermal Response Audiometry

This test involves a conditioning procedure that pairs a tone with a mild electric shock, which automatically changes the sweat glands of the skin. When the individual is conditioned, the shock is removed, whereas the sweat glands continue to change with the introduction of the tone. The subject need not respond with a signal, since the change in skin

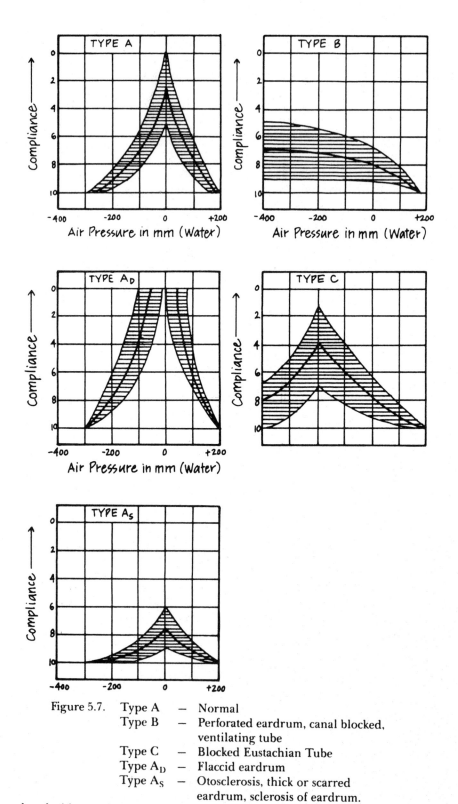

Figure 5.7.   Type A   —   Normal
              Type B   —   Perforated eardrum, canal blocked,
                              ventilating tube
              Type C   —   Blocked Eustachian Tube
              Type A$_D$ —   Flaccid eardrum
              Type A$_S$ —   Otosclerosis, thick or scarred
                              eardrum, sclerosis of eardrum.

resistance is automatically recorded on a graph. Because the test is frequently upsetting to a child, this type of evaluation is not often recommended.

Heart-Rate Response Audiometry

This test uses an electrocardiogram which measures the rate of heart-beat without the stimulation of sound and measures its rate after the presentation of a tone. Studies have shown that such testing can be effective; but it is very time-consuming and requires complete quiet on the part of the person being tested. As children are usually too active for this type of testing, it is generally confined to sleeping infants.

Electroencephalographic Evoked-Response Audiometry

This test records the changes in brain-wave motions when sound is introduced. Electrodes are attached to the skull to record brain waves while the child is at rest. Then, when sound is introduced, the results are recorded on a graph and the two conditions are compared. The difficulty here is that sounds must be well above threshold levels to obtain responses. As the sound approaches threshold, the recorded readings do not differ greatly from readings obtained when a child is at rest and no sound is introduced.

Electrocochleography

This test measures the stimulation of the nerve fibers of the Inner Ear with the presentation of sound. A needle electrode is inserted through the eardrum and placed on the bony structure of the Inner Ear mechanism. Clicks are introduced while electrical signals are measured within the Inner Ear. The test results, however, have required high-intensity levels of sound to be introduced, and the electrode must be inserted through the eardrum.

HEARING AID EVALUATION

The testing procedures followed by an audiologist fitting your young-ster with a hearing aid will be similar to the results obtained during the audiological evaluation. The difference is that the hearing aid, not the audiometer, makes the sound louder than normal. To determine how well the instrument is performing, its volume will be held at a constant volume while speech is introduced at normal loudness levels ("speech discrimination"). To determine how close to normal this is, the intensity of the speech can be decreased to find a level at which sound can just be heard ("speech-reception threshold"). We hope that this will be near that of a person with normal hearing. During this part of the testing procedures, sound is introduced through loudspeakers, while the child is wearing the hearing aid(s).

When an accurate audiological evaluation has been completed, the audiologist can compare and select from two or three instruments.

SUMMARY

There are a variety of methods used by the audiologist to determine the degree and nature of your child's hearing impairment. These techniques are accomplished through the use of special instrumentation so that your child can profit from appropriate medical attention or be fitted with a hearing aid that will maximize the remaining usable hearing. You should, therefore, become familiar with these measurements and their meaning so that you can fully understand the auditory potential of your youngster. Hearing aids, as you will learn through the next chapter, are not a cure. They are an aid to better understanding of speech and language through the auditory mechanism.

Chapter 6

HEARING AIDS

INTRODUCTION

If your child's hearing loss has been diagnosed as nerve deafness, your physician will surely recommend a hearing-aid evaluation, so that one or possibly two instruments may be fitted. You must then proceed immediately. Remember that your child may not have heard any sounds or only distorted speech without the use of a hearing aid. Children with normal hearing have been listening to speech and environmental sounds since birth. Most consistent hearing-aid users who suffered from hearing losses before they learned language have been fitted with their instrument from early infancy.

As you will be responsible for the care and maintenance of your child's hearing instrument during the initial stages of its use, you must be sure to understand its mechanical parts. This chapter, nevertheless, places greater emphasis on what the hearing aid can and cannot do, as well as the reasoning for its consistent use, regardless of the degree of impairment. If you can find an audiologist willing to take the time to help you, or if you refer to a number of booklets or brochures that are commercially available, the maintenance aspects can be learned quickly.

HEARING AID COMPONENTS

Hearing aids contain three basic components. The microphone receives airborne speech and converts it to electrical impulses. The amplifier increases the loudness level. The receiver converts the amplified sound to an airborne signal. Attached to the hearing aid is an earmold which directs sound to the ear canal (See Fig. 6.1). The chain of events described in Chapter 3 ("Physiology of the Ear") then occurs.

51

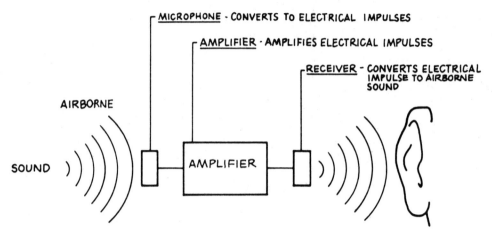

Figure 6.1. Diagram of three basic parts of any type hearing aid.

TYPES OF HEARING AIDS

Four types of hearing aids are available: body style, in-the-ear, behind-the-ear, and eyeglass (See Figs. 6.2, 6.3, 6.4, and 6.5).

Recently, much publicity has been given to the cochlear implant, which, incidentally, is not exactly new. In 1957, a patient underwent an operation that implanted an electrode designed to stimulate the acoustic nerve. The Outer, Middle, and Inner Ears were bypassed. The patient was able to speech read more efficiently but was unable to understand speech or other sounds clearly. Current surgical methods still do not restore the hearing, because the sounds that the individual hears are limited by the extent of nerve damage to the Inner Ear. Surgery may benefit those who:

1. cannot be helped by a hearing aid
2. are profoundly deaf in both ears
3. were at one time able to hear
4. have no other serious medical problems
5. have a family that is supportive
6. possess enough motivation

Currently, the electrode is inserted as shown in Figure 6.6, and attached to a microphone and speech processor which can be worn on the belt or in a pocket. This method of amplification has not yet been approved by the Food and Drug Administration for use with children.

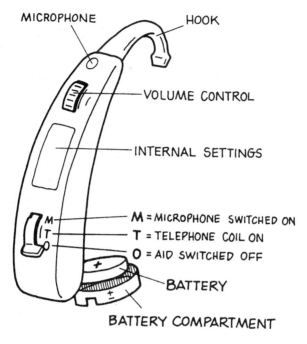

Figure 6.2. Labelled parts of a typical behind-the-ear hearing aid.

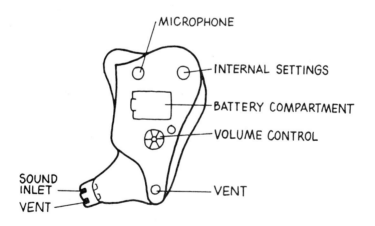

Figure 6.3. Labelled parts of a typical in-the-ear hearing aid.

Usually, in-the-ear and behind-the-ear instruments can be fitted for all but the most profound hearing losses, whereas body aids are sometimes recommended for infants or more active children. Since the parents are required to control and maintain the aid, it is often easier to

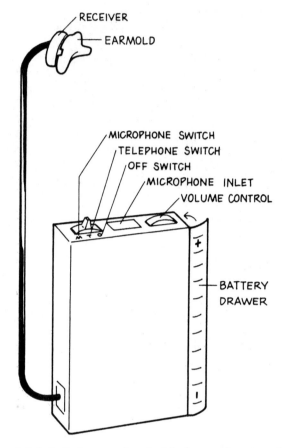

RECEIVER

EARMOLD

MICROPHONE SWITCH

TELEPHONE SWITCH

OFF SWITCH

MICROPHONE INLET

VOLUME CONTROL

BATTERY
DRAWER

Figure 6.4. Labelled parts of typical body-type hearing aid.

fasten, conceal, and set the controls in a body harness. In addition, it minimizes loss and damage, because it is far less costly to replace the receiver and earmold rather than the entire instrument. To fit the necessary amplification system behind a child's small Outer Ear has recently become less difficult, thanks to many manufacturers who are now producing instruments that are more powerful yet smaller in size.

HEARING AID FUNCTIONS

Naturally, your child should be fitted with an appropriate instrument. Speech should be heard at a comfortable loudness level and, of course, as clearly as possible. Most hearing aids now have settings so that the con-

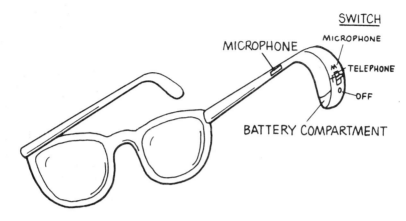

Figure 6.5. Typical eyeglass hearing aid with labelled parts.

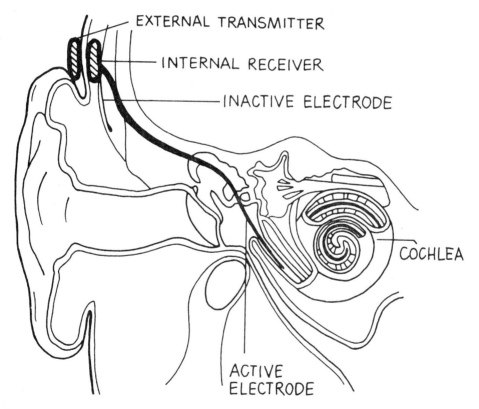

Figure 6.6. Insertion of cochlear implant showing the transmitter, receiver and active electrode inserted into the Inner Ear.

trols may be well regulated. Settings are specified in the form of a prescription by the audiologist, and should set forth make, model, and settings.

Maximum Power Output

No aid should permit greater output levels than your child can tolerate. Sound can cause discomfort or pain. Therefore, extreme care should be taken when levels of 130 Db are exceeded.

Gain

Comfort levels are more important than a threshold for hearing, for although an excellent threshold may be found, your child will simply not wear an aid if the sound is too loud. Left to their own devices, children will automatically reduce volume, in an attempt to adjust the instrument.

Frequency (Pitch Response)

Usually, a hearing aid should be allowed to amplify more high than low tones, because vowel sounds, as a rule, fall in the lower tones and provide the least understanding of speech, whereas higher tones provide the greatest amount of understanding of speech. Moreover, low tones carry more energy and tend to mask the higher tones.

CHOICE OF HEARING AID

This will depend upon the child's age and whether or not he or she is quiet or overactive. Infants are often fitted with body-type instruments to avoid loss, damage, added expense, or manipulation of control. Because of its efficiency, the aid of preference is a behind-the-ear, air-conduction instrument, created by the location of the microphone near the Outer Ear where we normally hear. Bone-conduction instruments may be used effectively when a child has a malformed Outer Ear or ear infections prevent blockage of the ear canal by an earmold.

Which Ear?

Generally, if one ear is better than the other, the better ear will be fitted. If, however, one ear is near normal and the other is more severely impaired, the audiologist may decide to try to fit the poorer ear to balance the hearing. If both ears have the same degree of loss, usually both are fitted. When one ear understands amplified speech far better than the other, the speech introduced to the poorer ear may detract from the overall quality. Research has proved that two ears function better than one, so binaural amplification is preferable whenever it is appropriate.

Dispensers

The audiologist should consider the scope of service available from the hearing-aid dispenser, bearing in mind the following:

1. Is he experienced in working with children?
2. Does he handle children well?
3. Is he responsive to your questions?
4. Will he lend your child an aid in case of damage or malfunction?
5. Are his prices reasonable?
6. Does he make satisfactory molds, and will he replace them at no cost if they are not correct?
7. Can you obtain a time-payment plan?
8. Will he offer some sort of trial arrangement?

Character of Aid

Your audiologist should consider how sturdy are the instrument's case and controls, and if it is of the right size. If it is a body aid, the microphone's location, hazards of spillage, and whether or not the case or prong inserts are sturdy should be taken into consideration.

By knowing something of what the audiologist knows you will be better equipped to ask intelligent questions.

HEARING AID PERFORMANCE

Normally hearing individuals rely largely upon their hearing for the understanding of speech and language, although speech reading, observation, and contextual clues are additional aids. Your child, to some degree, has been deprived of this opportunity and, of course, this has retarded the development of understanding as well as vocaliazation of normal speech and language patterns. Regardless of the degree of nerve damage, a properly fitting hearing aid can help to correct this deficiency.

Language is made up of a series of vowels and consonants. Spoken words are a blend of these sounds, with different combinations of vowels and consonants distinguishing one word from another. Vowel sounds tend to fall in the lower pitch range, carry the greatest amount of energy, and provide the least amount of understanding. Consonants tend to fall within the higher pitch range and provide the least carrying power and the greatest amount of understanding.

Unfortunately, all but the most profoundly deafened suffer more from nerve damage in the higher pitch range, where the greatest amount of understanding is found. Even with a hearing aid, amplified speech may still be distorted. When too many nerve fibers of the Inner Ear are damaged, speech will never be completely clear. Those who have more hearing in the low tones can be accommodated with hearing aids that provide amplification only in the higher pitch range. This will help equalize the loudness level of both high and low pitches. Of course, those with losses in both high and low pitches, as well as those with more severe hearing impairment, usually need amplification provided throughout the entire range of hearing.

Hearing and understanding are entirely different. Your child may hear sounds and speech through the use of a hearing aid but still not understand them, for an aid simply amplifies sound; it cannot replace damaged nerve fibers. How clear speech will be depends upon the extent of nerve damage. An aid makes speech loud enough so that it is within the individual's range of hearing. If the loss is milder, chances are that increased volume will permit excellent clarity. If, however, most of the nerve fibers of the Inner Ear are damaged, the wearer will hear speech and environmental sounds, but not clearly.

Nevertheless, speech at a comfortable loudness will provide your youngster with a greater degree of understanding, but as the extent of loss increases, the amount of information provided through hearing alone will be less. Although it is more difficult for a child with a profound loss to understand speech, any added bits of information are bound to improve his or her understanding. To interpret speech sounds, words, and sentences into meaningful wholes will require time and practice. Since there is no way of predicting how successfully he will perform, you must provide the opportunity as soon as possible. Many severely hearing-impaired children have learned to use their hearing in a supplementary manner, regardless of how distorted speech may be.

Never allow yourself to think that your child will not profit from a hearing aid. Consider ham radio operators, compelled to listen to speech that is frequently distorted or overridden by background noise. In time, practiced listening enables them to select meaningful bits of information, piece them together, and understand the communication. If you were to listen to the same messages for the first time, you would probably not understand much; but then, with practice, like the radio operator, you would probably achieve understanding. The mind is amazingly capable of adapting.

SUMMARY

This chapter was designed to provide you with some understanding of the basic components of all hearing aids, the various types of instruments available, and the mechanical parts with which you should become most familiar. It has also stressed the important role that your dispenser can play in assisting you and your child with the ongoing care and maintenance of the instrument. Finally, you have been provided with some understanding of what a hearing aid can and cannot do. Once you feel comfortable manipulating the aid and understand what *your* child is capable of hearing and understanding through its use, you will be better prepared to select the appropriate communication system that will be most beneficial to him for the development of language.

Chapter 7

PSYCHOLOGICAL EVALUATIONS

PURPOSE AND TYPES OF TESTS SELECTED

In addition to a physical, medical, and audiological evaluation, a psychological is a necessary part of the total process. Generally, it will provide you and the educational unit with two types of basic information:

1. It will help to determine your child's capacity to learn, especially in a school setting.
2. It will provide information on the developmental aspects of your youngster.

Both types of information are measured relative to other children, while taking into consideration the uniqueness of each child. Three major areas of concern are:

1. intelligence
2. neurological development
3. social/emotional development

Each of these will be discussed separately and some typical psychological instruments will be noted and described briefly.

Psychological evaluations are completed on older hearing-impaired children to determine achievement in the basic skill subjects:

1. reading
2. spelling
3. written expression
4. mathematics

Although they are a part of the psychological evaluation, they are usually administered by a classroom teacher, the counselor, or a resource room teacher. Occasionally, the psychologist will administer these tests, but it is often only a screening process, while the classroom examination is more detailed.

The instruments selected to evaluate your child will depend on his or her age and the extent of the hearing loss. If your youngster has a mild impairment and functions like a child with normal hearing through the use of a hearing aid, the testing procedures and battery of tests used may not be any different. On the other hand, evaluating a child with a severe or profound hearing loss will require special tests and techniques. Obviously, verbal tests would be rendered invalid if your youngster has not developed sufficient speech and language through oral methods alone. Therefore, the psychologist would not be accurately measuring your child's verbal skills, since the hearing loss may have prevented normal acquisition and use of language by the time the evaluation is completed. Thus, it is essential that the psychologist review the audiological, with and without amplification.

PSYCHOLOGISTS' SKILLS

Until very recently, psychologists did not receive training with special attention given to a hearing-impaired population. As a result, many youngsters were misdiagnosed by psychologists unfamiliar with special tests designed for children with a hearing loss. More often than not, instruments based on a normally hearing population were utilized. Only those youngsters who were seen by psychologists employed by private or state facilities where the entire student body had hearing impairments received an appropriate evaluation. These psychologists had learned the psychology of deafness and the appropriate instruments to use through on-the-job training and experience.

In addition, most psychologists employed by public education facilities were not familiar with the various communication systems necessary for the establishment of rapport or to provide explanations required to obtain valid test results. It was not uncommon for these youngsters to find themselves placed in classrooms with children who had other handicapping conditions. If they were more wisely referred to facilities where a psychologist was familiar with the appropriate test batteries and was equipped to communicate with the youngster effectively, the outcome was far more beneficial to the child.

Fortunately, since the passage of P.L. 94-142, training programs for psychologists have been greatly modified to include understanding of the psychology of the hearing-impaired and familiarization with the appropriate test batteries that will provide valid, accurate measurements. Since more of these youngsters are mainstreamed in classrooms for the normally hearing child, or have been placed in self-contained classes for the hearing-impaired, training programs for psychologists have been forced to address themselves to this issue. Also, psychologists who have been employed by the public sector have been required to learn appropriate communication techniques and test batteries especially designed for children with hearing losses.

In view of these circumstances, you should be cautious with regard to the skills of the psychologist who is assigned the task of evaluating your child. If he/she is unfamiliar with the available test batteries, does not have them available, or is unable to communicate with your child effectively, you should question the test results. As a parent, you have the right to inquire into the education, training, and qualifications of the psychologist who evaluates your child. By all means you should feel free to do so.

Some of the factors you should consider are as follows:

1. Is the psychologist state certified?
2. Does he/she have any experience working with hearing-impaired children?
3. Can the psychologist use manual means of communication?
4. Can the psychologist use tests which are appropriate for the age and degree of hearing loss of your child?
5. If you choose a psychologist who is a private practitioner, is he licensed by your state, and can he meet the qualifications as outlined above?

THE SETTING

The testing environment should provide conditions that are suitable for an accurate evaluation. The testing room should be well-lighted and well-ventilated, the office and testing furniture should be appropriate for the age of the child, and the office attractive, but distraction-free. During the examination, scoring the test results in the child's line of vision should be avoided. This can be distracting, thus affecting performance. If a pencil is necessary, the younger child should be provided with a primer-type for ease of grip.

Although you will be greeted in a waiting room, you should not expect to accompany your child while the tests are being administered. Most children will separate easily, so you should allow the examiner to take over while you urge your youngster to comply. If, however, you have travelled a long distance for the examination, the psychologist may request that you accompany your child. Although this is not preferable, since the presence of a third person in the testing room may be distracting and reduce rapport, it may be necessary so that the evaluation can be completed. If you are asked to accompany your youngster, you should seat yourself out of the child's line of vision and avoid participating in any way.

INTELLIGENCE TESTING

Despite disagreements that have been raised over the use of intelligence tests, they can provide the parents and educators with a useful tool to measure potential learning ability. This will depend upon their proper use and interpretation.

On the average, children at each age level are able to perform certain tasks and possess certain knowledge. As a result, a scale was devised whereby intelligence can be determined as well as mental age. This allows the examiner, parents, and educators a means by which they can see where a given child fits within his own age group.

The intelligence quotient ("I.Q.") arose out of the mental age concept. It is used as a measure to compare one child's score with those of a group of average children of the same age. In a simple formula it can be expressed as:

$$\frac{\text{Mental age}}{\text{Chronological age}} \times 100 = \text{I.Q.}$$

For example, if a child who is ten years old passes ten of the tests administered, his I.Q. would be calculated as follows:

$$\frac{10}{10} \times 100 = 100 \text{ I.Q.}$$

If he were to pass nine of the tests his score would be:

$$\frac{9}{10} \times 100 = 90 \text{ I.Q.}$$

Or, if he passed the tests designed for a twelve year old, the score would be:

$$\frac{12}{10} \times 100 = 120 \text{ I.Q.}$$

A different way of determining an I.Q. is by comparing the performance of a child with the average scores of a group of children of the same age level. The deviation I.Q. has an average of 100, with a standard deviation of ten to fifteen points for each age group. Still other tests can be expressed in percentiles. This compares your child with a group of children within the same age group. The 50th percentile is the average point. If your child scored at the 50th percentile, it would be equated with an I.Q. of 100. If he scored below the 50th percentile, his I.Q. would be something below 100; or, if he scored above the 50th percentile, his I.Q. would be above 100.

Intelligence Quotients are distributed in a normal fashion throughout the general population. Thus, 50 percent of the population falls above a 100 I.Q., and 50 percent below a 100 I.Q. level. The 50th percentile is the average point and can be compared with an I.Q. of 100. All of this can be graphically shown on a curve as follows:

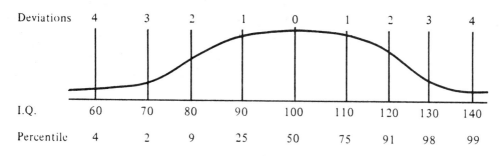

Deviations	4	3	2	1	0	1	2	3	4
I.Q.	60	70	80	90	100	110	120	130	140
Percentile	4	2	9	25	50	75	91	98	99

If an individual fell two standard deviations below the average he would be at the 9th percentile rank and have an equivalent I.Q. of 80. Should another individual fall two standard deviations above the average, he/she would be at the 91st percentile and show an equivalent I.Q. of 120. The intelligence level of your child can roughly be categorized as follows:

	130 +	-	Very Superior
120	– 129	-	Superior
110	– 119	-	Bright Average
90	– 110	-	Average
80	– 89	-	Low Average
70	– 79	-	Borderline
69	–	-	Mentally Retarded

You should remember that Intelligence Quotients can change since they may be influenced by learning experiences within the school setting, cultural level of the home, physical ailments, and so on. Since any such factors could influence the test results, you and the psychologist must consider how valid the results and conclusions reached may be.

As previously noted, the tests selected must be determined by the age of the child, the degree of hearing loss, and how well the youngster has acquired and is using language. Assuming a child is nonverbal, or his acquisition and use of language is limited by the hearing impairment, some of the typical test batteries are discussed on the following pages.

PSYCHOLOGICAL TESTS

Hiskey-Nebraska Test of Learning Aptitude for Young Deaf Children

This test gives the best results with children below the age of ten. It is particularly useful in that it provides norms for both deaf and hearing children. Therefore, it can be used to test more moderately hearing-impaired children who derive considerable benefit from amplification as well as those who are more severely impaired. The following subtests are found in this instrument: object memory, bead stringing, picture association, block patterns, picture completion, picture identification, paper folding, attention span, puzzle blocks, and picture analogies (See Fig. 7.1).

The test battery yields a learning age ("L.A.") which can be translated into a learning quotient ("L.Q."). The scores reveal strengths and weaknesses as well as interpretations made similar to an I.Q. This lends support to the idea that intelligence tests are a measure of learning ability and potential.

The Leiter International Performance Scale

There are two forms of this test currently in use. Both are nonverbal in nature. The test, as originally developed, extends from age two up to adults. Its particular advantage is that it can be used with a wide variety of individuals because the use of language is not required. The test is made up of a series of subtests, arranged by age groups, basically requiring matching skills. The test starts with very simple items, increasing in difficulty until the individual totally fails. A mental age is obtained and this is calculated into an I.Q. as previously noted by the formula.

This test was later standardized on a population between the ages of

Bead Stringing

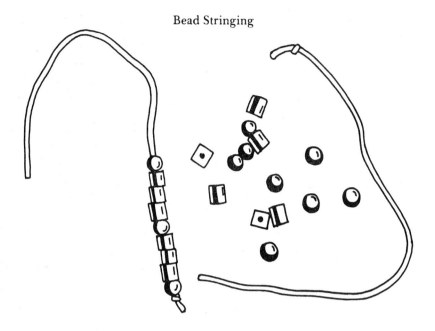

Picture Identification

Figure 7.1. Illustrations show the subtests, bead stringing and picture identification. Reproduced with permission of the author, Marshall S. Hiskey, University of Nebraska.

three to eight years of age using the same items. The major disadvantage of the test is that the items are relatively small, which is often troublesome for poorly coordinated young children (See Fig. 7.2).

Two-Year Level

Four-Year Level

Figure 7.2. Illustrations show a nonverbal subtest designed for two year old children, and one designed for four-year-old children. Reproduced with permission of the publisher, Stoelting Co., 1350 South Kostner Ave., Chicago, Illinois 60623–1196. Copyright, 1948. Rights reserved.

Merrill-Palmer Scale of Mental Tests

This test is designed for children in the preschool and primary grades. The battery includes nineteen subtests of nonverbal abilities. There are ninety-three test items that are ranked according to difficulty. The final score obtained can be interpreted in any one of three ways:

1. a mental age
2. finding the standard deviation after calculating an I.Q.
3. finding the percentile value of the score

This battery of tests permits observation of the child in three areas: neuromuscular development; social-emotional development; and general knowledge (cognition). The test materials are brightly colored and resemble toys rather than test materials, allowing for quick and easy rapport (See Fig. 7.3).

The Wechsler Tests

The three tests of the Wechsler are probably the most widely used intelligence tests. They are as follows:

1. The Wechsler Preschool and Primary Scale of Intelligence ("WPPSI") for children aged four to six (See Fig. 7.4).
2. The Wechsler Intelligence Test ("WISC–R") for children aged six to sixteen (See Fig. 7.5).
3. The Wechsler Adult Intelligence Scale ("WAIS") for children and adults aged sixteen to seventy-four (See Fig. 7.6).

These scales have a series of verbal and nonverbal subtests. Each test yields three separate scores: a verbal I.Q.; a performance I.Q.; and a full scale I.Q.

The advantages of these tests are that the examiner can elect to administer both portions of the test if the child is sufficiently verbal, in spite of the hearing impairment; or, administer the nonverbal portion only if the child is more severely impaired and nonverbal. The nonverbal portions of these tests have been standardized for a hearing-impaired population.

The Stanford Binet Test of Intelligence

Although this test is widely used among a normally hearing population, it is definitely not appropriate with hearing-impaired individuals. It has been standardized on the basis of a normally hearing population, and is heavily weighted in favor of the verbal child.

Sequin Form Board

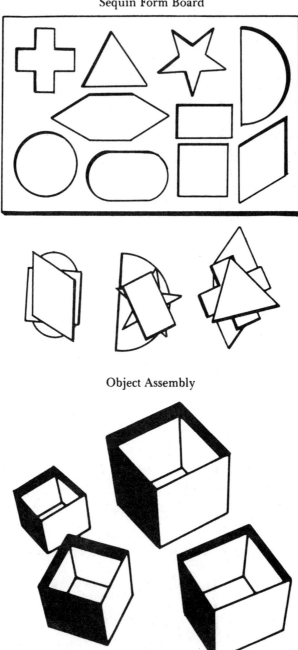

Object Assembly

Figure 7.3. Illustrations show the sequin form board and nested cubes, both subtest samples of the Merrill-Palmer scale of mental tests. Reproduced with permission of the publisher, Stoelting Co., 1350 South Kostner Ave., Chicago, Illinois 60623–1196. Copyright 1948. Rights reserved.

Picture Completion

Geometric Design

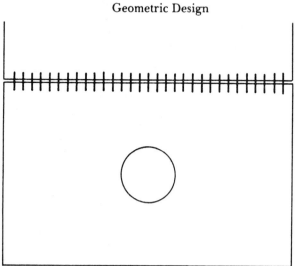

Figure 7.4. Two subtests taken from the Wechsler Preschool and Primary Scale of Intelligence. Reproduced with permission of the publisher, The Psychological Corporation, 555 Academic Court, San Antonio, Texas 78204–2498. Copyright ©1963. Rights reserved.

Block Design

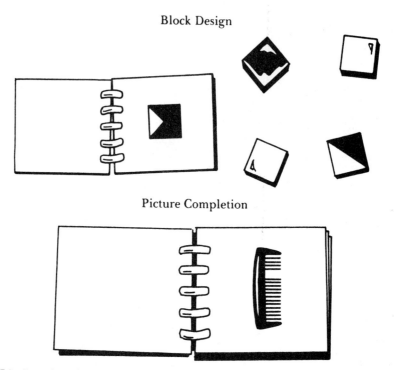

Picture Completion

Figure 7.5. Samples of the block design and picture completion tests of the nonverbal portion of the Weschler Intelligence Scale for Children—revised. Reproduced with permission of the publisher. The Psychological Corporation, 555 Academic Court, San Antonio, Texas 78204–2498. Copyright ©1974. Rights reserved.

DEVELOPMENTAL EVALUATION

The developmental evaluation is designed to obtain a measure of the child's social and emotional levels. There are both formal and informal methods of obtaining these measurements. They may come through the examiner's observation of the child and testing to determine how well the youngster performs certain tasks. In addition, the examiner may wish to question the parents through an interview technique or administer a more formalized battery of questions answered by the parents.

A number of factors are evaluated through these procedures such as the following; self-help skills, communication skills, self-direction, socialization, and locomotion skills.

House-Tree-Person and Human Figure Drawing

These tests are limited to older youngsters, but they can reveal some of the social and emotional aspects of your child's growth and development. Formalized testing of the hearing-impaired child, especially those more severely affected, is limited because of communication problems.

Vineland Adaptive Behavior Scale

This is the most widely used scale which can be administered on infants through adult levels. It is in the form of a questionnaire, and the parents act as informants. Items are listed in sequence on an age level progression. The total score or number of items which your child is able to perform is converted to a Social Age Level, and a social quotient obtained much like the formula used to determine an I.Q. score. The social quotient, however, may or may not be in accordance with the intelligence quotient (See Fig. 7.7).

Options to the Vineland Adaptive Behavior Scale are the Bayley Scales of Infant Development or the Scales of Children's Abilities, to name two.

Parent Conference

The parent conference should be a part of every comprehensive evaluation. This will assist the team of evaluators to arrive at better interpretations of test results and to make appropriate recommendations for your child's educational prescription. You should, therefore, be prepared to discuss your child openly and frankly, so that an accurate assessment of your youngster can be made. Probably, you will be asked to reveal information in three separate areas:

1. development history
2. medical history, and
3. family history.

If you are not offered an interview, you should insist upon one, since you can provide valuable information as to your child's growth and development. Also, the test results of the evaluation should be discussed with you. To gain some insight into the nature of the questions you might be asked, a typical outline has been included (See Fig. 7.8).

SUMMARY

This chapter was designed to provide you with some understanding of the significance and importance of the psychological evaluation, as well as the need for its accuracy in the diagnostic process. If it has been determined at an early age that your youngster has a hearing impairment that is noncorrectable by surgery or medication, special education may be a necessity. In the case of handicapped children, the accuracy of these evaluations is imperative so that your youngster can be placed in the most appropriate educational setting. Unlike normally hearing children, yours will probably begin this process at a much earlier age level.

Object Assembly

Figure 7.6. Two samples typical of the Adult Scale of the Weschler Intelligence Scale. Reproduced with permission of the publisher, The Psychological Corporation, 555 Academic Court, San Antonio, Texas 78204–2498. Copyright ©1981. Rights reserved.

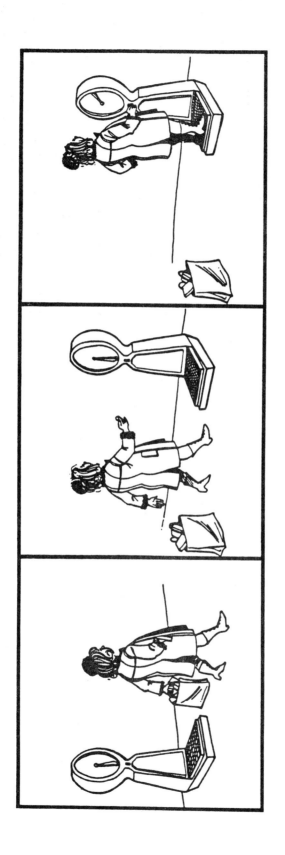

ITEM SCORES

2	Yes. usually
1	Sometimes or partially
0	No. never
N	No opportunity
DK	Don't know

RECEPTIVE   EXPRESSIVE   WRITTEN

COMMENTS

COMMUNICATION DOMAIN

		Item	
<1	1	Turns eyes and head toward sound	
	2	Listens at least momentarily when spoken to by caregiver	
	3	Smiles in response to presence of caregiver	
	4	Smiles in response to presence of familiar person other than caregiver	
	5	Raises arms when caregiver says. "Come here" or "Up"	
	6	Demonstrates understanding of the meaning of "no"	
	7	Imitates sounds of adults immediately after hearing them	
	8	Demonstrates understanding of the meaning of at least 10 words	
1	9	Gestures appropriately to indicate "yes," "no," and "I want"	
	10	Listens attentively to instructions	
	11	Demonstrates understanding of the meaning of "yes" or "okay"	
	12	Follows instructions requiring an action and an object	
	13	Points accurately to at least one major body part when asked	
	14	Uses first names or nicknames of siblings, friends, or peers, or states their names when asked	
	15	Uses phrases containing a noun and a verb, or two nouns	
	16	Names at least 20 familiar objects without being asked DO NOT SCORE 1	
	17	Listens to a story for at least five minutes	
	18	Indicates preference when offered a choice	
2	19	Says at least 50 recognizable words DO NOT SCORE 1	
	20	Spontaneously relates experiences in simple terms	
	21	Delivers a simple message	
	22	Uses sentences of four or more words	
	23	Points accurately to all body parts when asked DO NOT SCORE 1	
	24	Says at least 100 recognizable words DO NOT SCORE 1	
	25	Speaks in full sentences	
	26	Uses "a" and "the" in phrases or sentences	
	27	Follows instructions in "if-then" form	
	28	States own first and last name when asked	
	29	Asks questions beginning with "what," "where," "who," "why," and "when" DO NOT SCORE 1	
3, 4	30	States which of two objects not present is bigger	
	31	Relates experiences in detail when asked	
	32	Uses either "behind" or "between" as a preposition in a phrase	
	33	Uses "around" as a preposition in a phrase	

Count items before basal as 2. items after ceiling as 0   Sum of 2s, 1s. 0s page **2**

COMMENTS _____

_____

_____

_____

_____

_____

2

RECEPTIVE

EXPRESSIVE

WRITTEN

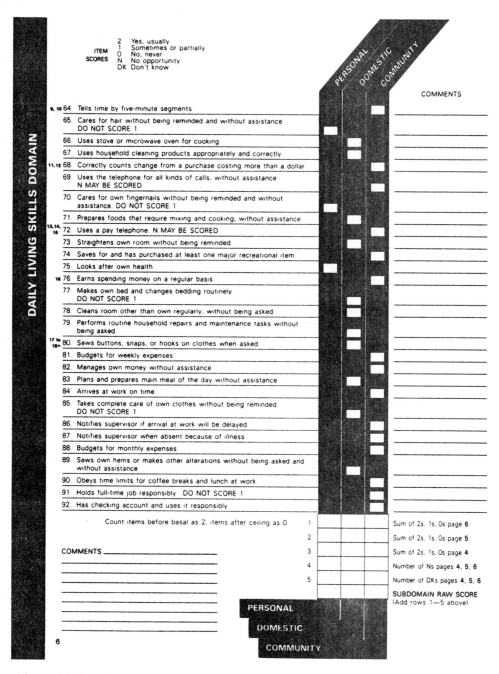

Figure 7.7. Sample pages of the Vineland Adaptive Behavior Scale with the parent or guardian acting as informant. Used by permission of the publisher, American Guidance Service, Publishers' Building, Circle Pines, MN 55014. *Vineland Adaptive Behavior Scales,* by Sara S. Sparrow, David A. Balla, and Domenic V. Cicchetti. Copyright 1984. Rights Reserved.

Name: Case No. _____
Address:
Date of Birth:

CONFERENCE WITH PARENTS

Siblings   Date of Birth   School   If Out of School
                                                Graduated   Work   Married   Children

DEVELOPMENTAL HISTORY

Parental Attitudes
  Father-
  Mother-
Pregnancy
  Difficulties
    Tense ☐   Anxious ☐   Sick ☐   Other-
  Infectious Diseases:
  Full Term: Yes ☐   No ☐   If no, how many months? -

Birth
  Length of Labor -   Delivery: Instruments   Yes ☐   No ☐
                                Normal ☐   Breech ☐   C-Section ☐

  Weight -
Feeding: Breast ☐   Bottle ☐   Schedule ☐   Hours?   Demand ☐
        Weaned: When?-
                 How?-
                 Reaction? -
Infancy
  Disposition -
  Degree of Activity: Normal ☐   Hyperactive ☐   Hypoactive ☐
  Eating -
    Problems at any time -
  Sleeping
    Nightmares ☐   Crying or Screaming ☐   Somambulism ☐
    Inordinate demands to come into mother's bed   Unusually early riser
  Colic   Yes ☐   No ☐   How long?

  Mother's physical, mental, and emotional state:

Developmental Tasks

    Teething-   Sitting Alone-   Crawling: Yes ☐   No ☐   Age -

    Walking-   Talking: Words-   Sentences-   Today-

                History of Difficulty-

    Toilet-Training: Age Begun-   Age Completed-

                Method:

                Reaction;

                Enuresis-   Encopresis-

MEDICAL HISTORY

Childhood Diseases	Serious Diseases	Others
Chicken Pox ☐ -	Diabetes ☐ -	
German Measles ☐ -	Encephalitis -	
Measles ☐ -	Epilepsey ☐ -	
Mumps ☐ -	Grand mal ☐	Petit mal ☐
Scarlet Fever ☐ -	Meningitis ☐ -	
Scarlatina ☐ -	Poliomyelitis-	

Whooping Cough-

History of Convulsions-

History of Seizures-

Black-outs or fainting spells-

High fever for more than 24 hours-

Accidents

    Broken bones-

    Head Injuries-

Operations

    Appendicitis ☐ -

    Circumcision ☐ -

    Hernia   ☐ -

    Eye   ☐ -

    T & A   ☐ -

    Other   ☐ -

    Doctors   Hospitals and/or Clinics

OB

T & A

Family

Other

FAMILY HISTORY

Paternal: Father   Alive ☐   Dead ☐ Cause of Death-

             Mother   Alive ☐   Dead ☐ Cause of Death-

             Siblings: Brothers-   Sisters-

                    Children Yes ☐ No ☐

          History of: Mental Retardation -

                     Emotional Disturbance -

                     Physical Disability -

Figure 7.8. Typical background history usually obtained during the evaluation of a child.

Maternal: Father   Alive ☐   Dead ☐   Cause of Death-
           Mother   Alive ☐   Dead ☐   Cause of Death-
           Siblings Brothers-   Sisters-
                     Children   Yes ☐ No ☐
                     History of: Mental Retardation -
                                   Emotional Disturbance -
                                   Physical Disability -

                        Father   Mother

Schooling-

Age

Occupation-

Health

Relationships
    Parents
       General Relations-
       Major Problems
    Siblings-
    Others (Adults and/or Children)-
Behavior at home-
Methods of Discipline-
    Done primarily by: Mother ☐   Father ☐
    Reaction-

STATEMENT OF THE PROBLEM ·
    Father-

    Mother-

ACCEPTED ROUTINE RESPONSIBILITIES

    What-
    Willingly and automatically ☐   Willingly ☐   Forced or Reminded ☐
    If none why not?

FRIENDS
    Making: Easily ☐ With Difficulty ☐
    Keeps: Yes ☐   No ☐   Intensive ☐   Extensive ☐
    Types: Same age ☐ Older ☐ Younger ☐ Same sex ☐ Opp. sex ☐ Both ☐
    School ☐   Neighborhood ☐   Both ☐
    INTEREST   HOBBIES   GROUP ACTIVITIES   FAVORITE TV SHOWS

OTHER PERTINENT INFORMATION –

                              INTERVIEWED BY _____
                              DATE   _____

Figure 7.8. *(Continued)*

Chapter 8

LANGUAGE DEVELOPMENT

INTRODUCTION

Language is a system of symbols that stand for things or ideas. It also includes a set of conventions, which are the rules that govern how these words will fit together in sentences. These symbols and conventions are arbitrary in nature, since they are devised by groups of people who have common interests.

Language is learned normally through the spoken word, assuming that individuals who communicate orally possess intact hearing and that they are able to speak each word in a fashion familiar to both. Ability to learn reading follows naturally through the printed form and then through writing. Spoken language, nevertheless, is not only the initial form of language development but also the foundation for its other aspects.

Language requires a sender and a receiver, and it is used by people who are attempting to communicate ideas in a precise manner. To communicate verbally, the sender and the receiver must understand it. If you were to visit an area where the language is different from the one you know, your ability to communicate will be seriously affected; in other words, you will not be able to express ideas or share common interests.

RULES

Every language contains a set of standard rules. These include the following concepts:

Vocabulary — The vocabulary is the group of words that are used in a language.

Grammar — This is the set of rules that governs the arrangement of words into sentences.

    1. *Syntax* — Word order.

2. *Morphology* — How words change their forms depending upon how they are used in a sentence — like or likes, dress or dresses, etc.

Semantics — This division of language concerns itself with the meaning of the sentence, and how we express this meaning by saying the same thing in two different ways.

Normally hearing children develop language in an effortless way through exposure. They simply listen. The process may be summarized as follows:

DEVELOPMENTAL SEQUENCE

(a) From birth to about six months of age, infants will listen to language before beginning to approximate its parts.

(b) At about six months, their babbling becomes the first attempt at oral expression. Then the child is playing with sounds and experimenting with his own vocal cords. Eventually he will include only what he has heard and stored in his brain since birth.

(c) Several months following the onset of babbling, the child will begin to try sentences. By the ninth month, he will have developed a sense of pitch and intonation (sometimes expressing stress).

(d) At about one year, he will begin to utter single words ("pivotal words").

(e) By two years of age, he begins to connect words, leaving no doubt as to their meaning.

(f) By three years, he is speaking in short phrases and sentences.

(g) By the age of seven, he will have learned to articulate all sounds by listening and imitating.

CONSIDERATIONS FOR THE HEARING-IMPAIRED

For the child with defective hearing, the development of language may be difficult, if not an impossible task; without the ability to receive and store, the reception of language is seriously curtailed. Furthermore, absence of hearing prevents the necessary feedback provided by listening to one's own speech.

The entire process of understanding is usually affected in direct proportion to the degree and nature of the hearing impairment. Many defects can be corrected or modified through the use of medication, surgery, or a hearing aid; but if the loss is due to extensive nerve damage, speech may be severely distorted regardless of the sound's intensity (See Figs. 8.1 and 8.2).

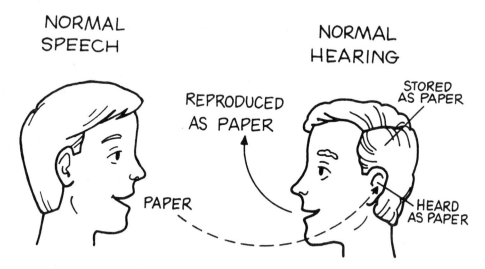

Figure 8.1. The expression, reception, storing and production of speech when both sender and receiver have normal hearing and speech.

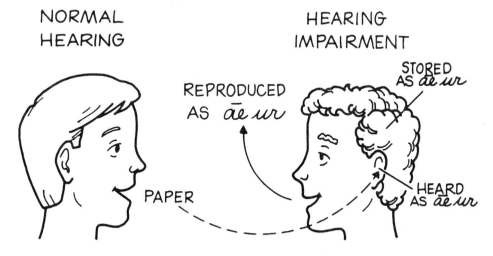

Figure 8.2. The production of normal speech by sender with defective reception, storing, and production by an individual with a sensorineural moderately-severe to severe hearing loss.

If a hearing aid proves inefficient, you may conclude that language reception could be acquired through speechreading, but it may be only a partial solution. Speechreading entails lipreading, close observation of facial expressions, and attention to "body language." Unfortunately 40 to 50 percent of the sounds of the English language are not visible. Also efficient speechreading requires an extensive language background. This allows an individual to fill in the gaps that are not provided otherwise through speechreading or hearing. Your child may have missed part or all of this opportunity because the hearing impairment has prevented proper exposure to language.

If you have ever attempted to learn a foreign language, you may recall the difficulty of this task, especially if you were confined to a classroom setting where the type and extent of exposure to the language limited your skills. Had you visited an area where the language was spoken by everyone, you would have learned its rules far more rapidly and accurately by listening to and duplicating them with your own speech. Depending upon the degree of the child's hearing impairment, learning language may be more like a classroom situation taught orally.

Early exposure is a key issue. Normally hearing individuals receive language in an effortless manner from the time of their birth. Once formal education has begun, most of the rules are intact. The hearing-impaired child may have acquired only a few, if any, and, of course, this creates a handicap from the outset. Because many of these children do not acquire language through hearing, speechreading and actual speech, they are taught to communicate manually.

SUMMARY

The goal is to devise a communication system which will expose the child to language on a consistent basis. The system will vary with each child, depending upon the type and degree of his hearing loss, the degree to which the loss can be corrected, motivation, speechreading skills, parent interest, knowledge of the child's skills, and ability to be flexible.

It may be that your initial choice does not work out but keep in mind that the system must effectively provide the child with language. However, it is merely a tool and language development is the key issue.

Chapter 9

SPEECH AND HEARING

INTRODUCTION

Since speech is the major avenue through which we communicate, as well as the initial source of our language development, the acquisition of speech is of concern to every parent who has a child with a hearing loss. Therefore, you should know something about its parts, how its sounds are produced, why some are more difficult than others to hear, and how a nerve-type of hearing loss can limit your youngster's expressive and receptive language skills. To what degree, of course, will depend upon the extent of damage, whether or not other handicaps are present, and the child's age when the impairment occurred.

SPEECH CHARACTERISTICS

Words are a combination of speech sounds, one blending with another. They are produced by forcing air from the lungs, past the vocal cords, and through the vocal tract. By positioning the articulators (lips, tongue, and teeth), different speech sounds are produced (Fig. 9.1), and these can be described by the placement of the articulators or if they are voiced or unvoiced.

Voiced and Unvoiced

When the vocal cords vibrate to produce a sound, the speech is voiced. Unvoiced sounds are produced without vibrations of the vocal cords. Vowel sounds are divided into two classes:

Pure Vowels

ee	heat	ah	father
i	hit	aw	call
e	head	u	put
ae	had	oo	cool

uh   the   ton
er   bird

Diphthongs

ou   tone
ei   take

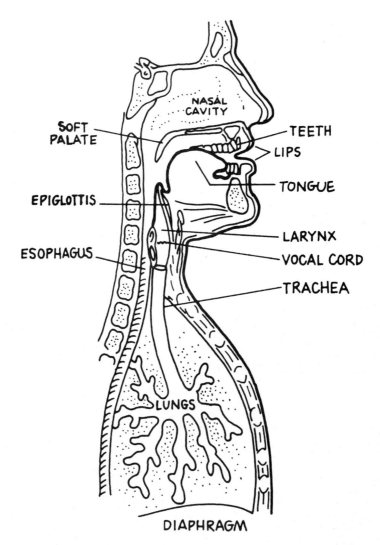

Figure 9.1. Parts of the head, neck, and chest essential to the production of speech. Illustrations from The Speech Chain, Peter B. Denes and Elliot N. Pinson. Copyright ©1963 by Bell Telephone Laboratories, Inc. Reprinted by permission of Doubleday, A Division of Bantam, Doubleday, Dell Publishing Group, Inc.

ai   might

au   shout

aim   toil

The quality of pure vowels remains the same throughout the syllables in which they are used. Diphthongs change their quality from the beginning to the end of a syllable; nevertheless, all vowels are voiced.

Consonants are divided into five different categories, but some of them are voiced, whereas others are unvoiced.

Plosive		*Fricative*		*Semi-Vowel*	*Liquids*		*Nasal*
p	b	f	v	w			m
t	d		th				
k	g	s	z	y	l	r	n
		sh	zh				
		h					ng

If you sound out each of the consonants, you will discover how some are voiced and others are unvoiced. Since many of them are unvoiced, they carry less energy than the vowels.

Placement of The Articulators

The differences between vowel sounds, whether pure or diphthongs, are modified by the position of the lips, and to a lesser degree by the position of the tongue. Consonants, on the other hand, are best described by placement of the lips, tongue, and teeth. They are more narrowly defined as follows:

Labial — placement of the lips

Labio-dental — placement of the lips and teeth

Dental — placement of the teeth

Alveolar — placement of the tongue on the gum ridge covering the teeth

Palatal — placement of the tongue against the roof of the mouth

Velar — placement of the tongue against the soft palate at the back of the mouth's roof

Glottal — the sound is produced by the vocal tract

Formants

The vocal tract leading from the vocal cords to the mouth also has an effect on the characteristics of speech sounds. It has certain frequencies (pitches), of which speech is a combination of many, that the tract is more responsive to than others. These are known as formants, or resonant frequencies, whose intensity is increased at these points. Each individual has slightly different resonant characteristics, depending upon the length and size of the vocal tract.

Each speech sound contains a fundamental formant, which is the lowest frequency of the speech sound, and harmonics, that are whole-number multiples of the fundamental formant. The second and third formants, or harmonics, of the sound, carry less energy than the first.

The pitch of a person's voice will be determined by the vocal cords. The more they are stretched, the higher the pitch. Formants do not change, however, since they are determined by the vocal tract. Most sounds can be heard clearly when three formants are within the range of hearing (See Fig. 9.2).

Speech Intensity

The loudness of speech sounds will vary around an average point, which is known as an average intensity level for speech. Blended together to form words, the intensity of each sound will fluctuate from one speech sound to another. For example, a voiced vowel sound will produce more energy than an unvoiced consonant sound (See Fig. 9.3).

The average intensity level of speech sounds varies between 55 and 65 Db, covering a frequency range of 50 to 10,000. However, most of the essential formants fall between 200 and 5,000 frequencies. Formants peak at certain frequencies. While the first formant appears at the lower end of the frequency range and produces more energy, the second and third formants fall at higher frequencies carrying less energy than the first.

Vowel sound fundamentals are located toward the lower end of the frequency range, while consonant fundamentals fall closer to the mid-range. Higher frequencies of the English language, however, provide the greatest amount of understanding. Yet this range is where most individuals have their greatest hearing loss. Thus, high-pitched voices are more difficult to hear than those that are low-pitched.

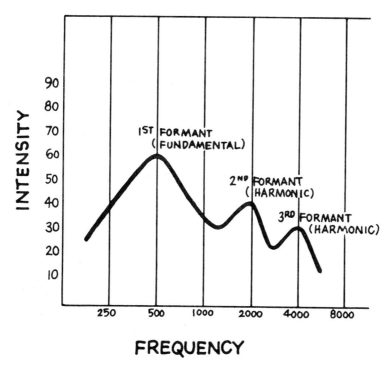

Figure 9.2. Shows the 1st, 2nd and 3rd formants of a speech sound, allowing clarity for most speech sounds.

If speech is delivered to a normal ear at an intensity of approximately 60 Db, all speech sounds will be heard and understood. As its intensity decreases below this point, understanding diminishes (See Fig. 9.4).

Vocal Sounds Following A Consonant

Sometimes a speech sound can be recognized in the absence of the second and third formant. This will be affected by speaker expectations, speaker familiarity, knowledge of grammar, the subject matter discussed, and the vowel sound following the consonant. The initial consonant sound often differs from another when it is followed by two different vowel sounds, even though the two consonant sounds may have nearly the same fundamental frequency. Thus, the p sound may be distinguished from an f sound if the vowel that follows is different.

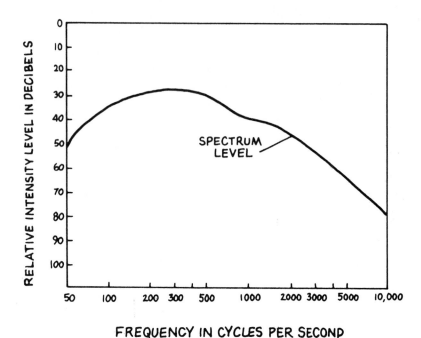

FREQUENCY IN CYCLES PER SECOND

Figure 9.3. Intensity levels produced by the various speech sounds of the English language. Vowels fall at the lower end of frequency range, with consonants falling at the higher range. Illustrations from The Speech Chain, Peter B. Denes and Elliot N. Pinson. Copyright ©1963 by Bell Telephone Laboratories, Inc. Reprinted by permission of Doubleday, a Division of Bantam, Doubleday, Dell Publishing Group, Inc.

Duration of Sound

If a two-syllable word is spoken, it is possible to distinguish one meaning of the word from another, by the stress placement on the first or second syllable:

Óbject   — stress on the first syllable
Objéct   — stress on the second syllable

As shown, the word changes its meaning when the stress moves from one syllable to another, even though the spelling remains the same.

Absence or Presence of Sound

In the presence of noise, normal ears will maintain complete understanding until background noises equal the loudness of speech delivered to one ear, or slightly exceeds the loudness of speech delivered to two ears.

HEARING SPEECH

Since most hearing impairments show a greater loss in the higher frequencies, hearing and understanding the English language is more difficult than others. In an earlier chapter, it was noted that consonants fall within the higher frequency range and provide the greatest amount of understanding, while vowel sounds fall within the lower frequencies, and provide the least amount of understanding. Vowels serve largely as carriers from one consonant sound to another; thus, the frequency range that the human ear requires for greatest intelligibility usually suffers from the most damage.

Depending upon the degree of nerve damage, consonant sounds may be made sufficiently loud, but clarity may be no greater. Even though the first formant, or fundamental, is within the range of hearing and understanding, the second and third formants, or harmonics, may not be heard at all. Remember, the second and third formants carry less energy, but they are usually necessary for the understanding of speech. Therefore, the sounds that provide the greatest amount of understanding are those that are most likely to be more severely distorted or beyond the range of hearing.

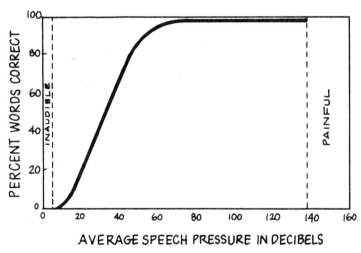

Figure 9.4. Line graph showing how speech becomes more intelligible as its loudness level increases. Illustrations from The Speech Chain, by Peter B. Denes and Elliot N. Pinson. Copyright ©1963 by Bell Telephone Laboratories, Inc. Reprinted by permission of Doubleday, a Division of Bantam, Doubleday, Dell Publishing Group, Inc.

Provided the nerve fibers of the inner ear are only partially damaged, reception of speech through hearing alone can prove most beneficial. If too many of the nerve fibers of the Inner Ear have been destroyed, hearing and understanding will be greatly reduced. These individuals will often require other methods of communication to acquire language. This may include speechreading, gestures, reading, writing, or some form of manual communication.

If your child has been diagnosed as hearing-impaired at an early age, it is often difficult to determine how effectively language will be acquired through hearing and speech alone. This leaves you one of two choices. You may wish to take the advice of professionals who have had years of experience with other hearing-impaired children; or you can make a decision based upon your own knowledge and experience. Regardless, the critical issue is whether your child is developing receptive language skills appropriately. In their absence, it is unlikely that your child will develop expressive language either.

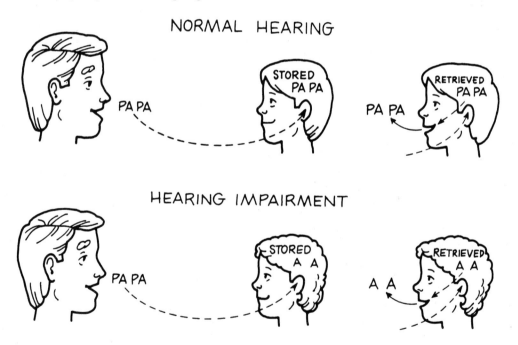

Figure 9.5. Shows the receptive and expressive language skills as a function of normal or defective hearing.

SPEAKING

If your child is unable to hear and understand speech, its production will be just as difficult. Infants who have normal hearing listen to speech for an extended period of time before they speak intelligibly. First, they practice the elements of speech by babbling those sounds that have been stored and retrieved from memory. Then they pattern their speech by monitoring its accuracy through their own hearing. This is referred to as the feedback process. If your child is unable to hear accurately the speech of others, the feedback mechanism will also be defective. This process is shown in Figure 9.5.

SUMMARY

Assuming there are no other complicating factors, such as mental retardation, brain damage, or physical defects affecting the articulators, most children with hearing impairments will derive some benefit from hearing. The basis for measuring your child's success or failure, however, should be determined by how well he or she is developing language. If it is at the same rate as children with normal hearing, there is no reason to resort to other methods of communication, since you and/or a speech correctionist can improve your child's speech and auditory perception through speech lessons, auditory training, and speechreading. If your child is not developing language at a normal rate, you may elect to combine speech with one or more of the methods described in Chapter 10.

Chapter 10

COMMUNICATION SYSTEMS

INTRODUCTION

There are a variety of communication systems from which you might wish to select. Your choice, nevertheless, will be dependent upon a number of considerations that are based upon your child's distinctly separate needs. Some of the factors that you should consider are: the degree of hearing impairment, whether several rather than one handicap is involved, your child's ability to lipread or speak clearly, and your willingness to learn new skills.

More importantly, the method should be chosen on the basis of language acquisition, and which system will allow your youngster to become a well-integrated member of the family and society. As the hearing-impaired child's contacts extend beyond the immediate environment to a more formal educational setting, these considerations will be even more critical and broader in scope.

The learning process takes place largely through the degree to which we acquire, expand, and manipulate language. Although we learn about our environment through all five senses—touch, taste, smell, vision, and hearing—vision and hearing, by far, dominate the other three. Denied of hearing, the communication process is interrupted. This deficiency will vary from one individual to another, based upon the age of onset and degree of damage to the hearing mechanism. Not only will it affect the child's skills in receiving and understanding language, but it will alter the youngster's ability to express it in an understandable fashion. This will foster the enrichment of experiences, allow for thought transmission, and enhance skills of reading and writing.

You should treat all of the following methods as tools, a means to an end, not an end in themselves. What may be correct for one child may not be for another. While one youngster may do well exposed to a pure oral method, another may require supplementary finger spelling. Still another may need a simultaneous approach to receive language clearly.

Therefore, it is important for you to choose the method that will best accommodate your child. Also, he or she should be permitted to express language in a way that is intelligible to you. Since you know your youngster better than anyone else, your understanding of the various methods of communication can help you sort and select which one or combination of methods is most appropriate.

The important issue is that you choose a method as quickly as possible, especially if the hearing loss has been incurred before acquiring language. Language development for the normally hearing child begins at birth. Your youngster missed some, a great deal, or all oral exposure due to the hearing impairment. Speech and language have been heard by your child in a softer, sometimes distorted manner, or not at all. His or her reception of language has been further limited by the lack of visual contact, while children with normal hearing have heard and understood language without this disadvantage. In the absence of sufficient hearing, the hearing-impaired child usually needs visual clues to aid understanding.

Try not to take a timid approach, fearful of making a mistake. If your initial decision for the choice of a method seems to be ineffective, be flexible and adapt it to suit your child's needs. Your youngster is suffering from the impairment, not you. You need to meet his or her needs, not yours.

What follows is a description of various methods of communication, which were devised to supplement a child's hearing deficiency. They are not presented as an argument in favor of one or the other. This is a conclusion that you must reach through first-hand knowledge of your child, conversations with professionals, observation of the methods in operation, and articles or books on the subject.

PURE ORAL METHOD

This method requires that normally-hearing and hearing-impaired individuals express language through speech and natural gestures that are commonly used and understood by almost everyone. The only device used to assist the deafened individual is a hearing aid. If this is insufficient to provide intelligible speech and language, the remainder is gathered through speechreading, facial expressions, or natural gestures. As the child's language facility begins to improve, reading and writing are added.

FINGERSPELLING (THE ROCHESTER METHOD)

This method uses all of the techniques employed by the pure oral method. In addition, twenty-six finger positions representing each letter of the alphabet are used to spell every word exactly as it is spoken in Standard English. Fingerspelling is delivered simultaneously with the spoken word, so that the person receiving language can fill in the gaps created by their inability to speechread or hear speech accurately. The adoption of Standard English by the hearing-impaired individual is the basic goal of this method (See Fig. 10.1).

SPEECH
+

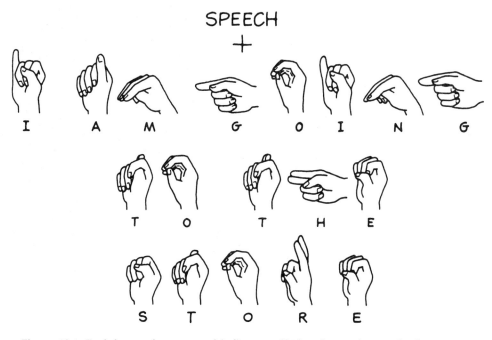

Figure 10.1. Each letter of every word is fingerspelled as the sender speaks the sentence.

SIGLISH (SIGNED ENGLISH)

All of the methods used by the pure oral and fingerspelling approaches are included in this communication system. In addition, the language of signs is incorporated, which is a combination of hand and arm positions or motions representing whole words. Standard English is still maintained, but the combination of methods allows for rapid transmission of words

and sentences in a manual and oral fashion. Since the English vocabulary far exceeds the number of signs available, this method still relies
heavily upon fingerspelling, so that Standard English can be maintained
(See Fig. 10.2).

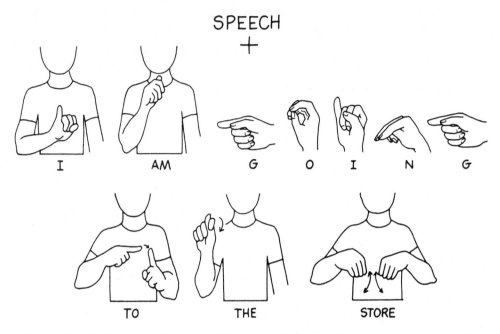

Figure 10.2. Both signs and fingerspelling are used to allow for more rapid transmission
of language. Standard English, however, is maintained.

AMSLAN (THE AMERICAN SIGN LANGUAGE)

This method makes no attempt to follow the structure of Standard
English. Signs are used almost exclusively, while word order, articles,
and tenses are changed or disregarded, singular and plural are considered as one and the same, and oralism is virtually excluded. Since it
makes no attempt to parallel Standard English, it is basically a method
designed to convey thoughts. Therefore, it is considered as a language
separate to itself (See Fig. 10.3).

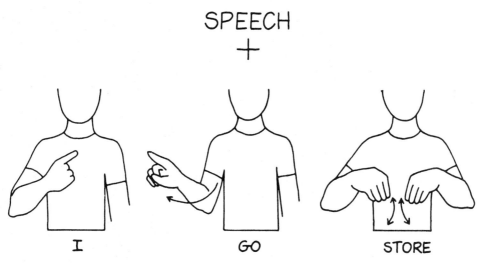

SPEECH

+

I   GO   STORE

Figure 10.3. Example demonstrates how the thought is conveyed while disregarding word order, articles, or tenses.

SIMULTANEOUS APPROACH

This method makes use of Amslan, while the word order of Standard English is maintained. Changing words to agree with the rest of the sentence—like to likes, go to going, and stop to stops—may be omitted. This method also extends the use of fingerspelling because of the limited number of signs (See Fig. 10.4).

CUED SPEECH

Cued Speech combines speech with eight hand shapes and four hand positions. Each hand shape represents three or four consonant sounds (l, s, k) that do not look alike, while each hand position represents vowel sounds that do not look alike. The purpose of this method is to offer cues so that the hearing-impaired individual can select the proper sounds within the context of the spoken sentence. Since only 40 percent of the English sounds are visible on the lips, it provides visual clues that supplement what cannot be heard or seen accurately (See Fig. 10.5).

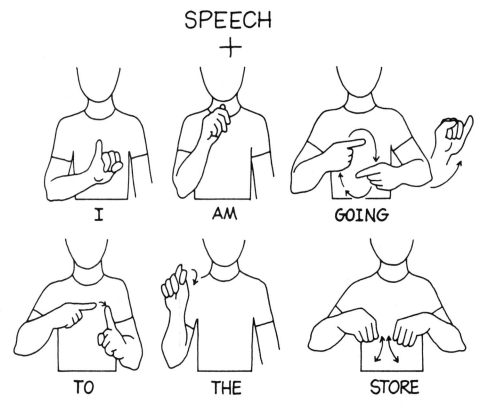

Figure 10.4. This approach shows the signs maintaining the word order. The sign for "ing" may be used or omitted at will.

TOTAL COMMUNICATION

Total communication has been included in this chapter to avoid confusion. It is not a method, but rather a philosophy. It suggests the use of any or all of the previously mentioned methods based upon the circumstances and the needs of the hearing-impaired individual; there-fore, it requires that the normally-hearing individual possess a working knowledge of all methods of communication. Based upon individual needs or the particular environment, the appropriate method is selected for use.

Although there are a variety of other communication systems that, with slight variation, fall within one of the categories described in this chapter, many simply carry another name. No doubt there will be many other methods developed, since there is continual research taking place.

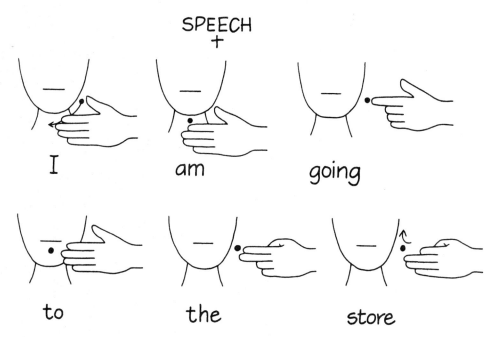

Figure 10.5. Visual clues to assist an individual to speechread invisible sounds produced while communicating orally.

Nevertheless, those methods that have been described encompass all of the major ones currently in use.

SUMMARY

If it has been determined that your child is suffering from a permanent hearing loss prior to the acquisition of language, it is important for you to decide which communication system you and your youngster are going to use. Although you may wish to discuss these matters with professionals or visit programs that employ each of the methods, be careful how you evaluate your observations, or what you are told. Communication systems have been and always will be a subject of considerable controversy. Whether this is due to a lack of understanding, preferences that have developed through the influence of training programs, or actual experience, caution on your part is wise. You know your youngster better than anyone else, so the final decision should be one with which you feel most comfortable.

Chapter 11

SPEECH, SPEECHREADING, AUDITORY TRAINING AND MANUAL COMMUNICATION

INTRODUCTION

If your child has incurred a hearing loss that cannot be treated medically or surgically, the only device that will assist with better understanding of speech from an auditory (hearing) standpoint is some type of amplification system. How much benefit will be derived will be determined by the extent of nerve damage suffered. Those children with milder impairments will, in all likelihood, hear and understand speech more nearly like normal through milder amplification; while others with more severe to profound losses will hear speech and environmental sounds in a somewhat distorted fashion even through the use of a powerful amplification system. However, remember that amplification systems simply amplify sounds, they do not clarify them. This is a function that the ear and brain stem must be capable of performing.

Should you discover that your child falls within the latter category, it may be necessary for you to resort to supplementary methods of communication to better insure your youngster's understanding of language. These methods may include speech, speechreading, auditory training and some form of manual communication. Although speech is the normal avenue through which human beings translate or convey thoughts, it may not be the only or primary manner through which your child will accomplish this task.

Whereas the child with normal hearing is able to receive language in an effortless manner by listening to its sounds and patterns, the hearing-impaired youngster may never be able to enjoy these benefits. Moreover, without language, the learning process will be retarded. By restricting your child to one mode of communication, you may be limiting him or her through no fault of their own. Your goals should be based upon an accurate diagnosis of your child's handicap(s), practical experience, your willingness to be flexible, and effort on your part to offer your child the opportunity to learn language through whatever means possible.

Regardless of the different approaches suggested, every child is unique. Your youngster's needs can be evaluated only in an individual manner. They should not be compared with other children who seem to be of a similar nature, since each child is an individual in his or her own right. Although they may appear to be similar, such may not be the case. In the absence of research, you are more well-advised by those who suggest that you use an adaptable communication method, of which speech, speech-reading, auditory training, and manual communication may be a part. This will offer your child the maximum opportunity to acquire language.

SPEECH

Under another chapter entitled Speech and Hearing, the mechanics of speech development was discussed with an explanation of how this process is translated when an individual is affected by a hearing impairment. Speech, however, is the initial means through which human beings develop language. In short, it is the norm which is accepted by most as a means to this end. Much of your child's success in this respect will depend upon the degree of hearing impairment, which provides most of us with a mechanism that will allow us to listen to its parts and pattern our speech through a monitoring process. This process is guided by how we hear our own speech. For some hearing-impaired children, the solution is simply to fit the child with amplification and what was once interrupted becomes a speech chain, connected and unbroken. Language, through oral avenues of communication, becomes complete.

Unfortunately, many hearing-impaired youngsters find that the development of language through speech is not quite so simple. If your child does not hear speech distinctly, he or she will not speak it clearly. If their hearing is partially damaged and they do hear it, they may speak it, but in a form to which you and other individuals with normal hearing are not accustomed. This does not negate attempts to develop speech, regardless of your child's hearing impairment. Since the human being relies upon speech so heavily, it seems appropriate to urge its use as much as possible.

For your child to learn language, speech becomes one of many communication systems available to your youngster. One must assume that if the potential exists, then it should be developed to its fullest so that your child can become as fully integrated with the general population as possible. On the other hand, if it is found that your child is unable to develop these skills, in spite of educators' or your efforts, you might wish to supplement it with some form of manual communication. In fact, you may conclude that a combination of all methods of communication is most suitable for your youngster.

There are a variety of methods that can be used to develop a hearing-impaired child's speech. These may include vibro-tactile (feeling the speech vibrations), music, hearing, syllable drill, and visual display of speech. Usually they are used in combination with one another. These techniques can be employed in a contrived classroom situation, during specified times with a speech teacher, or at home in a real-life situation. You should not, however, assume that your child will achieve as well as another, at the same rate, or less than another. Much of this progress will depend upon a variety of factors such as other handicaps, your efforts, and that of your youngster's teachers, as well as your child's natural ability. For example, some children can learn to engage in a sport and do extremely well; others may do fairly well but never become professionals, while still others learn only the basics of the sport, regardless of the amount of coaching they might receive. Rarely do you find an individual willing to try who cannot learn anything about a sport if he is physically able and is sufficiently stimulated to succeed.

You need to review periodically the situation regarding your child's speech development so that you can determine its effectiveness in terms of acquisition of language. You may need to modify your communication system so that it includes a more visible means for your child to receive and express language in all of its richness and beauty. Wishing it will happen through speech alone may be a senseless exercise on your part. This does not suggest that you exclude the effort entirely. Many most severely hearing-impaired individuals develop intelligible speech. Although its quality and quantity may be more limited than that of someone with normal hearing, it can prove most useful with the development of your child's language.

SPEECHREADING

It has often been stated that speechreading is an art rather than a skill that can be developed through concentrated effort. Whether this is true or not is an argument that will not be resolved in this chapter. You will have to make these judgments based on your own experiences with your child. Since it is difficult to predict levels of speechreading skills, there are certain aspects of this process which can be described. If you understand how speechreading may become an integral part of your youngster's language development, while you also understand its limitations, you should be more willing to concentrate some of your efforts in this direction.

Visual focus of attention is, with rare exceptions, directed toward the face. Even when manual communication is employed, this seems nearly always to be the case. It is as though we sense that there is some purpose and meaning attached to a speaker's lip movements, facial expressions, and eye contact. Indeed, even those individuals with normal hearing unconsciously speechread. If the child is hearing-impaired and a combination of communication systems is selected for use, the manual aspects will be digested through peripheral (away from the central part) vision.

Speechreading in the past was referred to as lipreading, as though all understanding through this manner of communication were to be obtained through lip movements. This philosophy was eventually challenged because of its obvious limitations, and a broader term, speechreading, took its place as a more accurate definition. Speechreading, unlike lipreading, not only includes lip movements, but also incorporates facial expressions, eye movements and body gestures. All of these parts tend to add meaning to a speaker's communication with another individual or group of people.

In the absence of clearly defined speech patterns, the hearing-impaired individual may find speechreading to be a valuable supplement to better understanding of oral language. You will notice that it has been described as a supplement and not a substitute for the absence of hearing. This is because speechreading has certain limitations of which you should be aware:

1. Approximately 50 percent of speech sounds are not visible on the lips, i.e., g, h, a, k.
2. Some sounds are homophonous (look alike on the lips) and are only distinguished from one another by their sound (p, b, m).
3. Those persons with a good language background tend to be better speechreaders.

If your child's hearing loss was incurred prior to the development of language, he or she lacks the necessary language background to initially speechread successfully. However, if the loss is of a mild nature, considerable language input may have taken place through your child's residual (remaining) hearing. This is a distinct advantage. This does not, however, suggest that speechreading should only be considered with the more mildly hearing-impaired child and its use denied to those children whose hearing loss has been evaluated as severe or profound.

Some individuals will suggest that speechreading and other oral techniques are the only methods of communication that should be considered. Likewise, some will recommend that oral techniques are insufficient or futile efforts, while manual methods are the better choice. Then you will find other parents and professionals who admit that there are no clear-cut answers, so you should try whatever seems appropriate for your child.

In the absence of predictive measures, you will need to consider the following:

1. The nature and extent of your child's hearing loss.
2. Your experiences with your child since early infancy.
3. What you have determined seems to be the most effective manner of communication with your child.
4. In spite of the hearing loss, you should try to determine whether your child is using this avenue of communication to receive language.

These will be issues that must be resolved when you consider a communication system for your child, as well as various program offerings when formal schooling is implemented. In the meantime, you can incorporate speechreading skills in your daily activities without the use of formal lesson plans. These may include visual attention and association of objects or activities with speechreading.

AUDITORY TRAINING

Auditory training, much like speechreading, may offer your child additional cues or clues toward better understanding of language. It, too, may have its limitations, depending upon the type and extent of the hearing loss. Your child's hearing impairment may leave only a few gaps, but, if the loss is of a more severe nature, none of someone else's speech may be distinguishable. Nevertheless, the most skilled professional is unable to evaluate how much or what quality of speech is being heard until your child is older. Once language has been developed, these measurements can be determined in a more accurate manner.

Although your youngster may only be able to distinguish the presence of some speech sounds, the use of auditory training still can be a useful tool toward the development of language. If a child with normal hearing is able to interpret various combinations of speech sounds into meaningful words, phrases, and sentences, your hearing-impaired child may be able to do likewise through a different set of sounds than those to which the normal ear is accustomed. For instance, the normal ear may listen to a particular sound and hear it precisely as does another normal ear. The hearing-impaired ear, however, may hear the sound, but in a way in which the normal ear is unaccustomed. Hearing and understanding oral language is essentially an identification process. If the child is able to identify what he hears with a certain word, it matters little just how the sounds making up the word are heard. Indeed, the learning process may be similar to that of a child with normal hearing.

Depending upon the degree of hearing impairment, the difficulty of learning language through hearing will be determined by its type and extent. Through the use of amplification, it may be possible that your child will develop language skills, through the assistance of amplification devices, in an oral fashion. On the other hand, some speech sounds may never be heard by your child regardless of the use of the most powerful aids. These gaps, such as those that are found in speechreading, will be ever present. The auditory (hearing) avenue may, therefore, be only a partial solution to your child's communication needs; but this does not suggest that you should abandon its use entirely. Indeed, you are more well-advised to consciously make an effort to use the method in the most effective manner possible.

There are a host of auditory training lessons available for the use of parents. Not unlike speechreading, you can accomplish many of these activities informally within the environment of your home or surrounding neighborhood. Basically, auditory training moves from more gross type sounds (police siren, fire alarm, pots and pans, door slamming, etc.) to the more complex sound differences created by speech. As one progresses in the development of these skills, language can be easily incorporated in this process.

MANUAL COMMUNICATION

It may be that you will wish to consider some form of manual communication to supplement your child's loss of hearing. Under a separate chapter entitled Communication Methods, the nature of these systems is briefly described. Keep in mind that they have all been devised to assist your child with the reception and expression of language. Although they cannot be treated as though they are the complete answer to your youngster's language problems, they can be a valuable resource. You may hear the argument that without manual communication, the hearing-impaired are doomed to failure. Others will argue that manualism will retard a child's oral skills. Both schools of thought are probably exaggerated and certainly are not supported by research or actual experience.

The advantages of a manual mode of communication are that they can, if utilized properly, provide a child with language in its complete form, through visual rather than auditory means. As far as their usefulness with a hearing population is concerned, they are all limited since most individuals are unable to understand or use any of them. Even so, it may be necessary for you to use one or more of these systems because your youngster needs them to acquire language. In any case, you will do well to select the communication system based upon what *you* know about your child. If language is not developing as normally as you might expect, or not at all, you might strongly consider a combined approach. If you were willing to accept the several forms of oral language development, which not everyone is, then why should you deny your child the opportunity of increased success through other methods of communication. If your child is nonoral despite your efforts or those of others, all of whom might be well intentioned, in your child's behalf you have the responsibility to allow him or her to become an individual in his own right.

Of course, you need to maintain oral techniques since they too will offer your youngster parts of the language structure as it is commonly used and accepted. Although your child is limited orally, there is no reason to despair or believe that all is lost. It is better that you spend more time on your child's strengths rather than on weaknesses. Should the strengths be nurtured to their fullest, your youngster will probably find a host of social and employment opportunities that offer an environment in which long-range comfort can be found.

In spite of criticisms that can be leveled at any communication system, manual methods seem to be a valuable tool to teach language to many children. If your youngster needs them, then it is not inappropriate. In the case of another child, it may be unnecessary. Either way, any of these systems may be invaluable to the child who is unable to acquire and use language through some form of pure oralism. It only becomes harmful when you or professionals treat it as an end-all. You may be denying your child the opportunity to acquire language through whatever means possible. This will only retard your youngster's habilitation. The hopes and desires that you might have created in your mind may be undermined by you and the professionals rather than by your child.

SUMMARY

Language development for a hearing-impaired child is often a difficult process. For some children, hearing aids alone may not be the entire solution to this problem. Speech, speechreading, auditory training, and manual communication, nevertheless, could be important tools for your youngster's language development. In the absence of sufficient research, coupled with inadequate predictive devices, there is no way to determine how well your child will develop these skills. Their effectiveness will be based upon your attitude, experiences, and effort in behalf of your child's accomplishments. One must presume that all methods might be of value to your youngster during the language learning process. For some, this will be a relatively easy task, while for others it may be more difficult. You will need to assume an attitude that it is better to have tried than not to have tried at all.

Any method, in itself, may not be the sole answer for your child. These questions will require your careful observation and your ability to modify your communication system. You have already learned language, but in the presence of a hearing loss, your youngster differs from you. Remember, what you might like to see happen may not meet your child's communication needs. Your efforts are better directed toward satisfying your youngster's requirements. He or she must learn to cope with the hearing impairment, not you. As you will find in the teaching of all subject matter, there is no single method that is appropriate for all children. If a method of teaching fails, a teacher will not cling to its use. Others will be tried.

Communication is not the central issue, the development of language is. Anyone can devise a communication system. Regardless of how limited it is, it will serve to meet one's basic needs. For your child to enrich his or her life, to blend with society at large, to find emotional stability, and to find employment and be successful at it, a command of language will be of the first importance. To deny any hearing-impaired child the opportunity to develop these skills will only prove to be a further handicap. Whatever combination of communication methods you choose, they should provide your child with language in its most complete and acceptable form.

Chapter 12

LEGAL ASPECTS

INTRODUCTION

All handicapped children between the ages of three and eighteen are entitled to a free public-supported education under the Education For All Handicapped Children Act (P.L. 94-142). Should the state in which you reside provide programs from birth to three years and eighteen to twenty-one, they should also offer the same for your child. These programs, of course, must be considered appropriate for your youngster. This may or may not be placement in one of the existing programs for normally hearing youngsters. If not, it is the responsibility of your local school district to devise an appropriate program, or to place your youngster in an existing one tailored to meet the needs of the handicap(s).

P.L. 94-142 contains a description of certain rights that you can exercise as safeguards for your child receiving any less than an appropriate education. Listed and described in the following sections of this chapter are the fundamental parts of P.L. 94-142.

RIGHT TO A FREE EDUCATION

It is the right of every handicapped child, and the obligation of every state, to provide a child with an appropriate education, at no cost to the parents. Prior to the enactment of this law, it was estimated that, of the seven million handicapped children reported, nearly three million were not receiving an appropriate program, or no program at all. If the necessary services are not available within the public school system, your school district must develop a program for your child, or fund one that is considered appropriate within the private sector. Regardless, you cannot be financially penalized because you have a handicapped child.

ASSURANCE OF EXTENSIVE CHILD
IDENTIFICATION PROCEDURES

It is the responsibility of your local school district to make provisions for the identification of all handicapped children living within their district, and to assist you with the completion of evaluations that are deemed appropriate. The school district may call upon county, state, or private agencies for assistance with these evaluations, but they should be accomplished at no cost to you.

ASSURANCE OF "FULL SERVICES" GOALS
AND DETAILED TIMETABLE

This provision requires that your child be offered the opportunity for placement in any one of the program options described in a later chapter entitled "Educational Options." The placement, of course, should be made on the basis of what is appropriate for your child. It also requires that supportive services—speech therapy, language therapy, auditory training, special tutoring, supplementary communication, physical therapy or psychological services—must be made available if it is determined that your child is in need of any one or more of these services.

GUARANTEE OF COMPLETE DUE PROCESS PROCEDURES

If, for some reason, the parents, educators, and evaluators are not in agreement with the suggested placement of a handicapped child, the parents have the right to request a due process hearing. These procedures follow more informal meetings where your child's program description is outlined and differences are discussed, but unresolved. Should you determine that these differences are irreconcilable, then your school district should advise you as to how to proceed with a due process hearing.

During the hearing, an impartial officer, usually appointed by the State Department of Education, will preside. If you wish, you may elect to hire a lawyer and/or expert witnesses to supply supporting evidence in favor of your position. You may also obtain independent evaluations; and, if evidence clearly indicates that the school district's evaluations are inappropriate, misleading, or inaccurate, your district is liable for their cost.

If you feel uncomfortable or insufficiently prepared to present your own case, it would be wise for you to seek assistance from others who are better prepared to defend your request for placement. Nevertheless, before you proceed with a due process hearing, you should search your mind with respect to your position, determine whether your request is reasonable, and be ready to support it with factual data. When differences between your school district and you arise, the burden of proof is yours, not the district's.

Once the Hearing Officer has heard all of the evidence, he or she will close the hearing without making a final decision. After reviewing the testimony, a brief will be written describing what he or she considers an appropriate program for your child. If the school district is able to make these provisions, then your youngster will be placed in their recommended program. If they are unable to do so, they will probably accede to your wishes. Once the program is implemented, it is the obligation of the Hearing Officer to determine whether his recommendations have been followed.

If you feel that you are still in disagreement with your child's placement, you have the right to appeal your case to a higher official, who is usually the State Secretary of Education. If this individual supports your school district, the decision is binding for a period of one year. Since you may continue to differ with the district, it is your right to initiate these same procedures during the next annual Individualized Educational Program planning conference.

ASSURANCE OF REGULAR PARENT OR GUARDIAN CONSULTATIONS

Through the Individualized Educational Program planning conference ("I.E.P."), and the teacher/parent conferences, you should be kept informed about your child's schooling. School districts vary concerning individual conferences. Nevertheless, you may always request more frequent meetings. If it is necessary for you to take the initiative, by all means do so. Since your child is handicapped, it is important for you to keep abreast of your youngster's progress. You need to have sufficient information available so that your child receives a continuum of programming that is appropriately designed. Otherwise, the educators will make all of these decisions for you.

ASSURANCE OF NONDISCRIMINATORY
TESTING AND EVALUATION

This provision of the law protects your child from misdiagnosis. If the evaluator is unfamiliar with the appropriate tools for correctly assessing your child's mental ability, academic skills, or emotional status, the test results will obviously be invalid. It is also important that the evaluator be equipped to effectively communicate with your child. This will better insure a comfortable working relationship, proper directions can be provided, and the evaluator understands any questions that your child may have prior to the administration of the tests. Misunderstandings can easily invalidate the test results.

GUARANTEES OF POLICIES AND PROCEDURES
TO PROTECT THE CONFIDENTIALITY OF
DATA AND INFORMATION

Each school district is required to maintain a set of regulations that specify how records of each child should be kept. Your youngster's records are confidential, so the district is obligated to request your approval before transferring information to another district or agency. Once your child leaves the district, the records must be purged and certain information destroyed. If you wish, you may obtain copies of any of your child's records, or you are free to visit the school so that you can read them at your leisure. Since these policies vary among school districts, you should contact yours to obtain a copy of their particular regulations regarding the maintenance of records.

ASSURANCE OF SPECIAL EDUCATION IN A
LEAST RESTRICTIVE ENVIRONMENT

The law is quite clear in this respect. This stems from the Least Restrictive Environment ("LRE") as outlined in the Federal Register (1976), Section 121a, 440 General, and is clearly the intent expressed in P.L. 94-142. The Register states that all handicapped children, to the maximum extent appropriate, should be educated with children who are not handicapped. Furthermore, it states that they should only be removed from such a setting when it is determined that the severity of the handicap is such that available support services and aids cannot be made available in the regular classroom. The law, however, provides safe-guards for your child. The program offered must be appropriate, a word often overlooked by school districts. If it seems appropriate for your child to be placed in a program option other than the general classroom, it should be made obvious through a program description, as outlined in the I.E.P. The program should be tailored to meet the child's needs, not visa versa.

MAINTENANCE OF AN I.E.P.
(INDIVIDUALIZED EDUCATIONAL PROGRAM)

Educators and evaluators must ensure that your child is receiving an appropriate program through the completion of an annual I.E.P. planning conference. The I.E.P. should clearly state the goals and objectives of all subject matter that will be covered for the school year. Each child must be reviewed by the staff and parents, at which time you should feel free to make specific requests for services or subject matter inclusions in your child's I.E.P. The I.E.P. serves as a document guide for the staff, insuring that from year to year your youngster receives a continuum of educational programming rather than a repetition of previously presented material. It is wise, therefore, for you to attend these conferences, since they establish the pattern for your youngster's education.

ASSURANCE FOR A SURROGATE TO ACT
FOR A CHILD WHEN NECESSARY

There are instances when a child lacks both parents. In such cases, it is possible for another relative or educator to be appointed surrogate to insure the child's rights.

IN-SERVICE TRAINING

Appropriate training programs should be established to ensure that all staff involved with your child have or are developing the necessary skills to identify, evaluate, develop I.E.P.'s and teach handicapped children.

ARCHITECTURAL BARRIERS

This aspect of the law requires that the architecture of the school setting be barrier-free. Such items as ramps, elevators, fire alarm lights, and other items should be installed to permit the child free access and protection.Also included under barrier-free removals is that interpreters for the deaf or readers for the blind should be made available if deemed appropriate.

SUMMARY

Public Law 94-142 has far-reaching consequences for your child, so you should become quite familiar with its contents. If you feel uncomfortable with the law, seek further clarification through your local school district's Director of Special Education. This individual should be thoroughly familiar with all of its parts, which will help to guide you to a clearer understanding of your child's rights.

Chapter 13

EDUCATIONAL OPTIONS

INTRODUCTION

According to Public Law 94-142, which has been described in a previous chapter, certain options are outlined for your child's education. These provide for the individual needs of youngsters who might have a wide latitude of skills and abilities. Although this chapter discusses these in the order of their appearance, the federal government does not suggest that they need be followed in any particular sequence. Rather, they urged that the child be exposed to any of these options after a complete evaluation of the youngster has been made, a description of the child's educational needs has been outlined, and a meeting has been held with the parents to determine their wishes.

The more informed you become regarding all aspects of your child's needs, the more influence you will have with educators and evaluators. Although they are responsible for the design of his or her program, you should be familiar with the options so that you can decide whether the one selected is appropriate. In all likelihood, they have called a meeting with you to urge you to accept a specific program. If you are unaware of what this involves, your youngster runs the danger of not receiving the full benefit of the suggested program.

PROGRAMS

Total Mainstreaming

Total Mainstreaming occurs when a hearing-impaired child is placed in a regular classroom setting with normally hearing children. Supportive services are considered unnecessary. Basically, the child is expected to function with children who do not have handicaps, in spite of the degree of hearing impairment.

Mainstreaming With Supportive Services

The hearing-handicapped child is placed in a regular classroom setting with normally hearing children. However, speech and hearing services are offered to offset the hearing deficiency. It is assumed that this assistance will enable the child to compete on a full-time basis in the regular classroom setting.

Resource Room

The hearing-impaired child is placed in a regular classroom setting in subject areas that are in keeping with children of a similar age and skill level. In addition, a self-contained classroom is provided to include special methods, materials, and staff that will assist him or her with tutorial services in these subject areas. If integration is considered impractical in certain subject areas, the teacher is prepared to manage these situations within the resource room.

Self-Contained Classes

Within a regular public school setting, classes are designed to accommodate more severely hearing-impaired children on the basis of academic levels, age, intellectual ability, and communication skills. It has been determined that these youngsters are unable to compete in the regular classroom in any of the subject areas offered because of their lack of sufficient oral skills, or they are functioning below grade levels expected of children of a similar age. Efforts are made to encourage the child to mingle with normally-hearing children through extracurricular activities in and out of the school setting.

Day Schools

These facilities are designed to accommodate only those youngsters who have hearing impairments. Like self-contained classes, they are grouped on the basis of academic ability, intellectual level, age, and degree of hearing loss. Because of the large number of students, grouping of the children is often more practical. Classroom integration is accomplished through nearby school systems, if it is considered appropriate. More often, it is expected to take place through family and neighborhood contacts.

Residential Schools

These schools are designed to provide for all of the child's needs, including academic, vocational, social, and emotional needs. These children are considered unable to communicate with normally-hearing individuals, and/or other handicapping conditions prevent their placement in any programs that have been previously described. Depending upon the population density, these youngsters are transported to their homes on a daily basis, every weekend, or during long holiday periods to maintain contact with the family.

Home Bound Instruction

When the child's needs are so complicated that it is not possible to transport the youngster to and from school, or he or she is unable to sustain a full day in a classroom setting, a home-bound instructor must be provided to teach the youngster, and to offer assistance with home management. If several handicaps are involved, other trained professionals are provided to offer these services.

Depending upon the population density of your area of residence, all of these options may not be locally available. You should contact the Director of Special Education or the Director of Speech and Hearing in your district or county to gain this information. In order for you to make sound judgments, you should discuss these matters with appropriate professionals.

PARENT ROLE

Once you have obtained the necessary facts, and have become aware of what programs are available, you can begin to determine which one you feel might be best for your child. Before you do so, it might be wise for you to formulate a few questions in your mind. For example:

How well-prepared am I to deal effectively with my child's hearing impairment?

Do I wish to be one of the major factors in my child's development?

What is my child's intellectual ability?

Does my child have other handicaps that will require special attention?

What is the extent and nature of my child's hearing impairment?

How well is my child communicating and in what way?

What are my child's language skills as compared to a normally hearing child?

How well-adjusted is my child?

In spite of my wishes, what program seems to be most appropriate for my child?

If factual information shows that my choice of programming is not suitable, am I prepared to modify my thinking?

How involved do I wish to become in my child's educational process?

SUMMARY

After learning more about your child and the programs available, you will feel much more comfortable with the decisions that are being made. Even more important, you will be better prepared to provide valuable advice regarding the accomplishments of these goals. Your knowledge of your child is probably as extensive as that of evaluators and educators. Although you may not be able to express it in technical terms, the fact that your child has lived with you since birth places you at an advantage.

Armed with an open mind, knowledge, and a clear understanding of your child's needs, you could be the principal party in determining what program will maximize your youngster's potential. Although you may feel inadequate and apprehensive because of the risks involved, it is better to take them. If you fail to do so, someone else will make the decisions for you.

Chapter 14

INDIVIDUALIZED EDUCATIONAL PROGRAM PLAN (IEP)

INTRODUCTION

Before passage of P.L. 94-142, the Education For all Handicapped Children Act, literally thousands of handicapped children were not receiving any type of education, the program offered was inappropriate, or youngsters received material that was a repetition of the previous year. In fact, nearly 40 percent fell into one of these categories. Meanwhile, parents were helpless, since they had little or no involvement in their child's education. Because they had no way of becoming a part of the plan's structure or design, their youngster was at the mercy of the educators.

Since the Individualized Educational Program Plan contains so many parts of P.L. 94-142, it has been expanded upon in this chapter. Adding to its importance, it includes the parents in its designing stage. For its proper development, all of the following aspects of the law must be considered:

1. Identification of the handicap(s)
2. Availability of optional programs
3. Support services
4. Due process procedures
5. Parent consultation
6. Testing and evaluation
7. Least restrictive environment

If you are familiar with your child's rights and you have an understanding of the impairment, you have an excellent opportunity to assist with the development of the program that your youngster receives. Through the IEP conference you will be given the chance to suggest or request that certain services or subject matter be included in his or her program. If your request is refused, you are entitled to a satisfactory explanation. If your suggestions are not unreasonable, usually you will find your district accommodating.

CONFERENCES

There are two major concerns during the IEP conference, the first involving the development of the program, while the second is your approval of the Program Plan.

Preplanning Conference

During the preplanning conference, the parents, teacher(s), program supervisor, audiologist (if one is available), and school psychologist, will meet with you to discuss your child's present education levels, determine what services will be provided, and generally outline instructional areas that will be covered. The instructional areas will include some description of the objectives for the year, what methods and materials will be used, and some means of evaluating these objectives.

You should be invited to make suggestions at the conference. To prepare yourself, it is important for you to understand your child's level of achievement, the nature and extent of the impairment(s), and your youngster's communication skills. It is your child that is involved, so feel free to participate.

Once the preplanning conference has been completed, your child's teacher(s) and the supervisor of the program will write the final draft of the IEP. In some cases this will be developed at the preplanning conference. If so, you may wish to sign the finished copy immediately, which will indicate your approval of the program. Some time later, you should receive a copy. If you do not wish to approve the Program Plan immediately, you may take a copy with you for further study. If the IEP developed during the conference is only a rough outline that requires final drafting, the school will send you a copy for review after it is completed. If you approve, you should sign it and return it immediately. You will find that schools vary in terms of their methods of managing these procedures.

If you are dissatisfied with any parts of the IEP, you should contact the program supervisor, indicating that you would like to see certain items changed, added, or deleted. If you are advised that the IEP will be modified, you should receive a revised copy for your approval and signature. Should any major differences arise, you should be advised of your Due Process rights, and the supervisor should outline how you can initiate these procedures.

Revision Conference

Once the initial IEP has been developed, each year thereafter a conference must be held to review your child's progress during the previous year, and to establish goals for the next school year. If it is necessary to modify or change the services offered, these matters will also be discussed. Again, you will be invited to provide suggestions, with the completed revision subject to your approval.

IEP CONTENTS

Each IEP contains three basic parts:

1. The face sheet
2. Present education levels
3. Instructional areas

Face Sheet

The face sheet of a typical IEP should contain the following items:

1. Your child's name and age
2. The location of the program
3. The primary assignment. For example, a self-contained class
4. The extent to which your child will have contact with normally hearing children
5. Additional services that will be received: psychological services, audiological services, physical therapy, physical education, or speech therapy
6. A beginning and ending date with a duration of one year
7. An anticipated date for review
8. The name of the person responsible for the supervision of the IEP

(See Fig. 14.1)

Present Educational Levels

The details describing your child's present educational levels will depend largely upon your youngster's age, but might contain any of the following:

INDIVIDUALIZED EDUCATION PROGRAM PLAN

Student's Name: _____

Birth Date: _____

Present Date: _____

Grade/Program: _____

Teacher(s): _____

District/School: _____

Primary Assignment(s):	Date Started	Expected Duration of Services	Special Media or Materials

Extent to which the
child will participate
in regular education: _____

Services: _____

IEP Planning Meeting Participants: Name

    Local Education Agency Representative: _____

    Parent, Guardian or Surrogate Parent: _____

    Teachers(s): _____

Date for review and/or revision of the Individualized Education Program Plan: _____

Person responsible for the supervision of the IEP: _____

Figure 14.1. Sample of the face page of a typical IEP.

1. Language skills
2. Communication skills
3. A level of functioning in mathematics, reading, science, and social studies
4. The grade level of text books used
5. Results of formal achievement tests

The facts stated on this page are the basis for your child's initial IEP, while each year thereafter they will determine what progress your youngster has made. It will also help you to decide whether the revised goals for the next school year are appropriate and logically sequenced (See Fig. 14.2).

Instructional Areas

Separate pages will be included in the IEP for each instructional area in which your child is receiving special education services. Each page will contain the following:

1. Instructional Area

This is the subject area of concern, such as language, reading, mathematics, science or social studies.

2. Annual Goal

The annual goal is a broad statement describing the general objective of each area. For example, it might state that your child will incorporate new vocabulary and language principles into oral, written, and signed language.

3. Short-Term Objectives

This part of the IEP describes more clearly what principles will be covered in each subject area. This might include learning new vocabulary and using the words in sentences, spelling new words, responding to questions, forming the past tense, identifying nouns, verbs, or adjectives, or writing in manuscript.

4. Instructional Methods

This section includes any materials prepared by the teacher, or textbooks that might be used during the course of the school year (See Fig. 14.3).

PRESENT EDUCATION LEVELS

Name_____

Present Date_____

Figure 14.2. Typical Present Education Levels page of the IEP.

Instructional Area: _____

Annual Goal: _____

Name _____

Present Date _____

SHORT-TERM OBJECTIVE	INSTRUCTIONAL METHODS MEDIA/MATERIAL TITLE(S) (OPTIONAL)	EVALUATION OF INSTRUCTIONAL OBJECTIVES	
		TESTS, MATERIALS EVALUATION PROCEDURES TO BE USED	CRITERIA OF SUCCESSFUL PERFORMANCE

Figure 14.3. Instructional Areas page(s) of IEP outlining the objectives, instructional methods and materials, and the evaluation of instructional objectives for the school year.[3]

5. Evaluation of Instructional Objectives

Under this section is a description of the types of test materials that the teacher will use to evaluate the success of your child's performance. This may include samples of your youngster's work, written tests devised by the teacher, tests accompanying the text, or standardized examinations available in each subject area.

The other area involved is the basis upon which the teacher judges your child's completion of the work. This may be through subjective evidence, as judged by the teacher, or a percentage level of performance.

SUMMARY

You should be aware that the IEP is not a legally binding document. Although a thorough evaluation of your child, an accurate description of present education levels, and a well-designed IEP should enable most children to successfully complete the objectives for the school year, they cannot be guaranteed. If the educators determine that your child is unable to deal with the stated goals, it is their responsibility to request another meeting with you to revise the IEP. Or, if you are carefully following your child's progress and determine that the work your youngster is receiving is inappropriate, you may wish to call for such a conference.

The IEP is a document that permits you to know what program your child will receive during the school year. In addition, it gives you the opportunity to participate in its development. If it is constructed properly, you should be able to trace the progress of your child from year to year; so by all means make every effort to take an active part in this process. It is your insurance that your child is receiving an appropriate education, so do not treat it lightly.

Chapter 15

POSTSECONDARY EDUCATION

INTRODUCTION

The attitudes of the American public have drastically changed toward postsecondary education during the past several centuries. What was once a highly agrarian society, gradually shifted to one that was more industrialized and mechanized. For political, economic, and social reasons, the past forty years have shown rapid movement of employees into service-type work. By the turn of the twenty-first century, it has been estimated that 75 percent of the workers will be spending their time servicing others, while only three percent will be engaged in agricultural pursuits, and 22 percent involved with the manufacture of goods.

During the late seventeenth, eighteenth, nineteenth, and the early part of the twentieth century, postsecondary education was developed through some of the finest institutions. They did, however, confine their curriculum to a liberal arts program in the main and appealed to an elite student body. It was presumed that a cultured man would ultimately become a leader in business, politics, or industry. The remainder of the work force was expected to learn on the job and to accomplish a degree of success through diligent, hard effort. This, of course, is an attitude considered intolerable and unpalatable by today's standards.

Until child labor laws were established during the early twentieth century, youngsters were not only expected, but forced to enter the labor market. Although many noted individuals advocated free public school education, economics demanded that it include first through eighth grades only. Children were needed to help with the chores, till the land, or labor in factories. Family sizes were considerably larger as compared to today. Money was scarcer. Hands-on labor was necessary to meet these needs.

At the turn of the nineteenth century, education for a hearing-impaired child was virtually nonexistent. These youngsters, unfortunately, were considered uneducable. In fact, they were commonly referred to as "deaf and dumb," more so because of their muteness than their intellectual liabilities. Most were relegated to household chores or menial tasks that required a minimum of communication skills.

Since the early settlers arrived, two hundred years passed before the initial schools for the deaf were established in the United States. The first was founded in Hartford, Connecticut, by Thomas H. Gallaudet, and named the American School for the Deaf, in 1817. Soon after The New York School for the Deaf was opened in 1819, followed by the Pennsylvania School for the Deaf in 1820. Since that time residential schools for the deaf have been established in nearly every state of the Union.

Most of the state-supported elementary and postsecondary schools for the deaf followed some form of manual communication during the early years. Their founders modelled these programs after methods devised by Abbe Charles Michel de l'Epee, who had developed the first finger alphabet, and opened a school about 1760 in Paris, France. Thomas Braidwood, a Scottish teacher, opened a school for the deaf in London, England, where he was said to have employed an oral method, but little is known about his techniques. The oral method flourished through the invention of "visible speech" by A. Melville Bell, of Edinburgh, Scotland. In 1871, Alexander Graham Bell brought his father's visible speech system to the United States and endowed the Volta Bureau at Washington, D.C. for the Increase and Diffusion of Knowledge Relating to the Deaf. Prior to that, the first school to use the oral method was the Clarke School for the Deaf founded in 1867 at Northampton, Massachusetts.

Since these early years, residential schools for the deaf have shifted from one communication system to another, with the exception of the Clarke School that has remained since its inception undeviatingly oral. During more recent years, it would appear that the simultaneous approach has been a reasonable compromise.

POSTSECONDARY EDUCATION

Gallaudet College, originally founded in 1857, has more recently adopted university status. Through federal legislation, the college was established as a liberal arts college for hearing-impaired students throughout the United States. Since it was the only college of its kind in the world, foreign students comprised a part of its student body.

In 1968, the federal government recognized a need to establish a more technically oriented institution for the deaf, known as the National Technical Institute for the Deaf ("NTID"). As an almost perfect complement, a site was chosen on the campus of Rochester Institute of Technology ("RIT") in Rochester, New York. This blend of facilities allows students to receive certificates, associate, baccalaureate, or graduate degrees from a combination of the two institutions.

Gallaudet, unlike NTID, for many years enjoyed a rather small enrollment. Between 1900 (107 students) and 1960 (350 students), it was attended only by the more advanced students. Most of the graduates entered the field of deaf education, returning to residential facilities that they themselves had attended. Since 1960, however, this has expanded in excess of 1,600 students. Gallaudet also operates two national demonstration programs: The Kendall Demonstration Elementary School, and a secondary program, the Model Secondary School for the Deaf ("MSSD"), has been added to include youngsters of the age of fourteen years and older. In addition, Gallaudet conducts graduate programs in the areas of School Psychology, Audiology, Counselling, Educational Technology and Social Services, Linguistics and an Educational Specialist or Doctor of Philosophy in Special Education Administration. Gallaudet also offers extensive courses at five other regional institutions.

NTID, however, has shown unprecedented growth because of employment demands, types of program offerings, and a wider range of subjects offered. Currently the enrollment exceeds 1,200, comprising a student body who receive certificates, associate, baccalaureate, and graduate degrees. Prior to this time, graduates of secondary programs received degrees that were backed by an emphasis on academic training. As a result, they found themselves less prepared to enter the general work force with saleable skills. NTID, on the other hand, continued to include liberal arts courses, but they stressed more technical subject matter.

During the 1960s, congressional legislation established four regional programs for the hearing-impaired, located on the campuses of colleges with a normally hearing student body. Because of the reluctance of students to relocate, these regional programs were made more attractive. Delgado Junior College, New Orleans, Louisiana; St. Paul Technical Vocational Institute ("TVI"), St. Paul, Minnesota; the Seattle Community College at Seattle, Washington; and Northridge at California State University were selected as the sites. Since that time, Delgado has been discontinued and the Post-Secondary Educational Consortium ("PEC") has taken its place at the University of Tennessee as the southern regional program.

In 1975, Section 504 of the Vocational Rehabilitation Act virtually revolutionized the field of education for the deaf. This Act legislated, by federal mandate, that all handicapped individuals be offered free access to programs receiving federal funds. As a result, the number of college level programs located in the United States and Canada that offer special services for the hearing-impaired increased to 145 by 1985, from a low of two in 1968 (See Figs. 15.1 & 15.2). In addition, the number of students with all degrees of hearing impairments rose to more than 11,000 by 1983. Approximately one-half attended on a full-time basis. This came about not only by the passage of Section 504, but by the desire of secondary students to broaden their educational and employment opportunities. It was also affected by colleges that began to compensate for their decreasing enrollment of hearing students throughout the United States. Of course, many of these students were attending colleges with little or no support services for the hearing-impaired. More recently, the Rubella epidemic has created a sharp increase in the number of hearing-impaired college students.

SERVICES OFFERED

As a parent of a hearing-impaired child, you should carefully consider your youngster's ability to achieve his or her goals through the college curriculum selected. This will be determined not only by your youngster's achievement levels, aptitudes, and interests, but also by the availability of the necessary services to compensate for the hearing loss. You must remember that although there are 1,000 colleges offering services to the hearing-impaired, these range from none to highly comprehensive services. Those colleges which devote their entire effort toward the education of the hearing-impaired student provide all of the necessary services, while others enrolling one or two students with a hearing loss assume that the youngster will be able to function in a classroom with little or no support (See Fig. 15.3).

Unlike a youngster with normal hearing, your child's choice of a college will require careful thought. You will need to understand fully his or her skills, considering the following services as related to your youngster's needs:

1. Individual tutoring
2. Special classes for the hearing impaired
3. Interpreting service

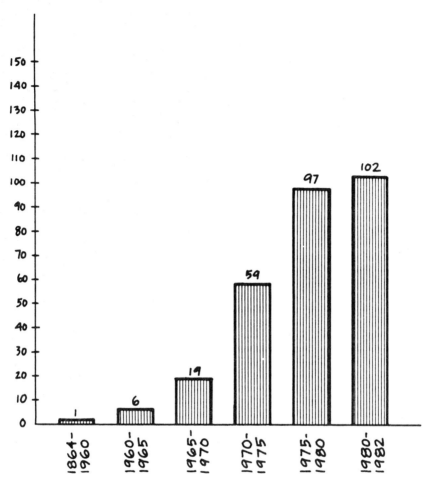

Figure 15.1. Breakdown of total programs for the hearing impaired through 1982. Figures used by permission of the publisher, College-Hill Press, San Diego, California 92105. *Deaf Children In America*, Edited by Arthur Schildroth and Michael Karchmer. Copyright 1984. Rights Reserved.

   4. Vocational counselling
   5. Personal counselling for hearing-impaired students
   6. Diagnostic service available
   7. Speech and hearing services
   8. Communication training for students
   9. Communication training for instructors
  10. Housing arrangements
  11. Social activities

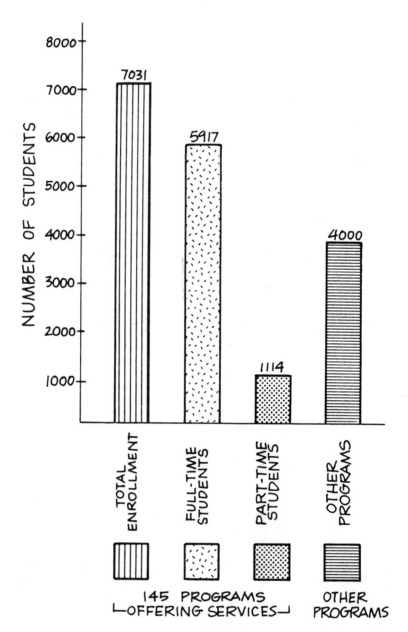

Figure 15.2. Total enrollment, full or part time, in colleges that offer services to the hearing impaired. Figures used by permission of the publisher, College-Hill Press, San Diego, California 92105. *Deaf Children In America*, Edited by Arthur Schildroth and Michael Karchmer. Copyright 1984. Rights Reserved.

Support Services	*All Programs* (N = 101)
Classroom Services	
Special class for deaf students	39
Interpreters (paid or volunteer)	98
Paid interpreters	90
Tutors	84
Notetakers (paid or volunteer)	93
Paid notetakers	53
Clinical and Counseling Services	
Vocational counseling	96
Counselors who sign	59
Personal counseling	96
Counselors who sign	64
Vocational placement	87
Counselors who sign	38
Speech and hearing clinical services	69
Services through program or host institution	32
Other	
Manual communication training for students	84
Manual communication training for instructors	81
Social and cultural activities	55
Preparatory activities	54
Supervised housing	47

Figure 15.3. Types of support services offered by 101 college programs. Figures used by permission of the publisher, College-Hill Press, San Diego, California 92105. *Deaf Children in America,* Edited by Arthur Schildroth and Michael Karchmer. Copyright 1984. Rights Reserved.

AREAS OF STUDY

Although schools for the deaf have historically trained their students in the manual arts, most of them offered skeleton courses, focusing most of their attention on the development of academic skills. Since the major handicap of the hearing-impaired is the lack of adequate language skills, the major emphasis was placed on this development. This situation continues to exist, with the exception of a few schools which offer a rather wide variety of trades.

Because students were graduating from secondary schools with only minimal skills, they found that employment opportunities were quite limited and sometimes nonexistent. This issue became even more complex, in that trade areas were becoming more technical in nature and required a great deal more in-depth knowledge. As a result, parents were frustrated by their inability to locate gainful employment for their children.

More recently, since 1960, legal reforms have broadened these opportunities through the opening of the regional programs, free access for the handicapped in schools traditionally designed for normally hearing individuals, and the implementation of appropriate services to meet their particular needs. Not only have the hearing-impaired been offered services of a nature previously described, but the career areas are vastly more comprehensive (See Figs. 15.4 & 15.5).

Career Clusters	1982 *Programs*
Total	23*
Agriculture	4
Business and office	22
Communication and media	17
Construction	8
Consumer and homemaking	10
Environment and natural resources	4
Fine arts and humanities	11
Health	7
Hospitality and recreation	11
Manufacturing	17
Marketing and distribution	1
Personal services	2
Product services	5
Public services	12
Transportation	10

*Clusters add up to more than 23 programs because programs generally offered more than one career cluster area.

Figure 15.4. Career selection offered by 23 college programs. Figures used by permission of the publisher, College-Hill Press, San Diego, California 92105. *Deaf Children in America,* Edited by Arthur Schildroth and Michael Karchmer. Copyright 1984. Rights Reserved.

SUMMARY

Postsecondary education for the hearing-impaired has shown unprecedented growth since 1960, as a result of federal legislation which has established regional programs and opened up opportunities at other colleges which previously were unavailable. The services, of course,

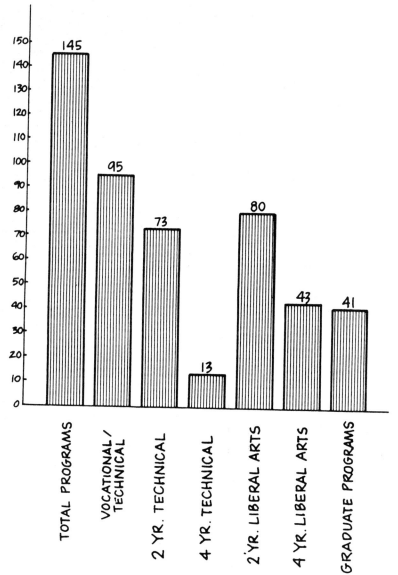

Figure 15.5. Numbers of postsecondary programs offering services for the hearing impaired by types of program. Figures used by permission of the publisher, College-Hill Press, San Diego, California 92105. *Deaf Children In America,* Edited by Arthur Schildroth and Michael Karchmer. Copyright 1984. Rights Reserved.

vary, which is a consideration that each parent and student must consider in light of the specific needs.

Because of technological advances and the absence of comprehensive and/or in-depth vocational programs offered by residential facilities or local school districts on the secondary level, many of the hearing-impaired children are now taking advantage of postsecondary programs. Needless to say, the growth of these programs has been unprecedented during the past twenty-five years, and will undoubtedly continue to follow a similar pattern in the future. Since basic language skills and academic subject matter are more slowly developed among the average hearing-impaired population, the major emphasis will be placed in these areas. This will require that more of these students pursue an education beyond the high school level.

Chapter 16

DEMOGRAPHICS

INTRODUCTION

Most parents who have been advised that their child has a noncorrectable hearing loss, regardless of degree, will experience concern in one or more of the following areas:

1. What was the cause of my child's hearing loss?
2. Since I do not know anyone else who has a hearing-impaired child, am I alone in my efforts to raise my child?
3. Will my child learn how to communicate effectively?
4. How will my child learn and how will he/she be educated?
5. Does my child have handicaps other than a hearing impairment?

These are but a few of the questions that may cause you concern if you are unaware of the facts. Therefore, the more information you accumulate, the sooner your fears will be arrested.

To gain perspective in this regard, you should have some knowledge of statistical data so that you can view your youngster's problem in relation to a larger population of youth with a similar handicap. For example, the distribution of the hearing-impaired population based upon degree of hearing loss, the causes of hearing losses prior to the acquisition of language, the distribution of youngsters who have more than one handicap, what types of schools these youngsters are attending, communication systems employed, speech intelligibility, and average achievement levels should be issues of concern to you.

The United States National Center for Health Statistics ("NHIS") and the Office of Demographic Studies ("ODS") conduct surveys periodically or annually regarding the hearing-impaired population in the United States. Although the following information is presented to offer you some basis of comparison, you should be reminded that your youngster is uniquely different from all others. Too many variables are involved for you to estimate where your child will fall in this spectrum.

GENERAL POPULATION

In 1974, a survey revealed that 840,000 youths between the ages of six and seventeen were estimated to have some degree of hearing loss. However, 487,000 of these had difficulty in hearing in only one ear, while 221,000 could hear and understand normal speech without amplification (NHIS). A second study, completed in 1980, which included youths between four and nineteen years of age, showed that 230,000 suffered losses greater than 26dB. Of these, 84,000 had a hearing loss of 41dB or greater, with an estimate of 14,000 with hearing losses greater than 91dB (NHIS) (See Fig. 16.1).

PERCENTAGE DISTRIBUTION BY AGE AND SEX
BASED ON BETTER EAR AVERAGE

All Students	Percentage Distribution			
(6–17 years of age)	All Levels	Under 41	41–90	90 and Above
	100.0	100.0	100.0	100.0
Age				
6–11 years	55.5	55.0	56.7	55.2
12–17 years	44.5	45.0	44.3	44.8
Sex				
Male	54.1	56.7	56.4	42.5
Female	45.9	43.3	44.6	47.5

Figure 16.1. Percentage distribution of hearing impaired based on age and sex. Figures used by permission of the publisher, College-Hill Press, San Diego, California 92105. *Deaf Children in America,* Edited by Arthur Schildroth and Michael Karchmer. Copyright 1984. Rights Reserved.

More recently, in 1981–82, it was estimated that 90,000 students are receiving instruction through special educational services for the hearing-impaired. Of these, 31,000 were classified as deaf, while 59,000 had lesser degrees of hearing loss (NHIS). Representative samples indicate how these youth are distributed based on special school or class attendance when the hearing loss is the major cause of limitation (See Fig. 16.2).

Gallaudet University devised a scale based on the degree of hearing loss and ability to understand speech. You should be aware, however, that this scale is based upon unamplified speech. With amplification, whether a youngster functions higher on the scale will be based upon a variety of

PROGRAM TYPE

	All	Special Schools or Classes
All youth—6–11 years	135,000	82,000
Age		
6–11 years	73,000	43,000
12–17 years	62,000	39,000
Sex		
Males	79,000	45,000
Females	56,000	37,000

Figure 16.2. Youth 6 to 17 years of age where hearing loss is the major cause of the limitation and attendance in special schools or classes. Figures used by permission of the publisher, College-Hill Press, San Diego, California 92105. *Deaf Children in America*, Edited by Arthur Schildroth and Michael Karchmer. Copyright 1984. Rights Reserved.

factors such as: when the hearing impairment was identified, when amplification was introduced, the type and degree of the hearing loss, the presence or absence of other handicaps and the effort to foster the child's use of his or her residual hearing. For example, it is possible for a child with a moderately-severe loss of hearing to function much like a normal hearing youngster if no other handicaps are present, amplification is introduced at an early age, and the use of hearing is stressed. If the nerve damage to the inner ear is not too extensive, the mind will adapt to distortions of speech that amplification alone cannot correct. If, however, the damage is too extensive, even amplified speech will, with few exceptions, require reinforcement through other methods of communication, i.e., speechreading and/or manual communication (See Fig. 16.3—*Deaf Children in America*, Schildroth & Karchmer, 1986).

ETIOLOGY (CAUSES)

The times or period of onset of a hearing impairment can be divided into three distinct categories:

1. prenatal—acquired prior to birth
2. perinatal—acquired at birth
3. postnatal—acquired after birth

Although causes are often clearly identifiable, there are a large number whose origins are unknown. If your child's diagnosis fails to reveal

DEGREES OF HEARING LOSS AND ABILITY TO UNDERSTAND SPEECH

Scale	Speech Comprehension Based on Better Ear Average	Better Ear Average
1.	No difficulty	Less than 26 dB
2.	Difficulty with faint speech	26–40 dB
3.	Frequent difficulty understanding normal speech	41–70 dB
4.	Only understand loud speech	71–90 dB
5.–8.	Cannot understand amplified speech	91 dB or more

Figure 16.3. Measured degrees of hearing loss and ability to understand speech. Figures used by permission of the publisher, College-Hill Press, San Diego, California 92105. *Deaf Children in America,* Edited by Arthur Schildroth and Michael Karchmer. Copyright 1984. Rights Reserved.

the cause of the hearing loss, you will service your child more effectively by avoiding issues of guilt and moving on to more productive ones that will remedy the defect(s). You are well advised to concern yourself with an accurate diagnosis and what the physicians, educators, and you can do to assist your youngster.

Even though the following statistics may provide you with an understanding of the many causes of a hearing impairment and how these youngsters distribute themselves, pay particular attention to the large percentage that fall into the unknown category. Regardless, it matters little to your child. It is more important for you to create an environment in which your youngster can feel comfortable and one that is conducive to his or her fullest development. Your attitude will be clearly reflected by your child (See Fig. 16.4).

MULTIPLY HANDICAPPED

The prevalence of handicaps among all school children is approximately 10 percent (U.S. Department of Education, 1980). Among hearing-impaired children, estimates of additional handicaps run as high as 30 percent (O.D.S.) as reflected in the bar graph (See Fig. 16.5).

Statistics indicate that between 60 and 70 percent of all youngsters with various degrees of hearing impairment have no additional handicaps, while approximately 30 to 40 percent suffer from one or more additional handicaps. Largely due to the Rubella epidemic of 1964 and 1965, the incidence of additional handicaps is greater among the older youngsters.

CAUSES OF HEARING IMPAIRMENT

Cause	Percentage
Unknown	39.5
Pre-Natal	
Maternal Rubella	16.3
Heredity	11.6
Meningitis	7.3
Otitis Media	3.0
Peri-Natal	
Prematurity	4.0
Pregnancy Complications	3.4
Trauma	2.4
Rh Incompatability	1.4
Post-Natal	
High Fever	3.1
Infection	2.7
Trauma	0.8
Measles	0.8
Mumps	0.2
Other	8.0

Figure 16.4. Figures used by permission of the publisher, College-Hill Press, San Diego, California 92105. *Deaf Children in America*, Edited by Arthur Schildroth and Michael Karchmer. Copyright 1984. Rights Reserved.

Barring another incident of this nature, the percentage should remain fairly constant as a result of the etiology.

COMMUNICATION SYSTEMS

As described in Chapter 10, there are a variety of communication systems available for use with the hearing-impaired. A study conducted during the years 1982–83 indicated that approximately 65 percent of hearing-impaired children used some type of sign language, while 35 percent did not. The survey further indicated that 98 percent of the students who used sign language were enrolled in programs where sign language, in one form or another, was incorporated in the educational program of instruction. Likewise, 92 percent of the students who did not use sign language were enrolled in programs that did not use signs as part of the methods of instruction. On the other hand, only 35 percent of the parents used sign language in the home while 65 percent did not (O.D.S.).

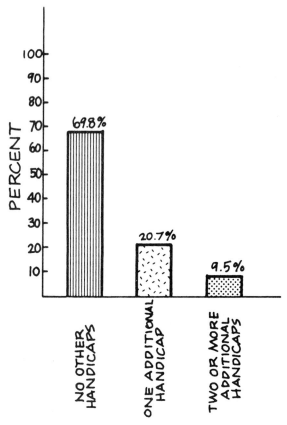

Figure 16.5. Numbers of hearing handicapped children with the presence of one or more handicaps. Figures used by permission of the publisher, College-Hill Press, San Diego, California 92105. *Deaf Children In America*, Edited by Arthur Schildroth and Michael Karchmer. Copyright 1984. Rights Reserved.

Although age, degree of hearing loss, ethnic status and age at onset of hearing loss are determining factors regarding a hearing-impaired child's use of sign language, the major determining factor seems to be whether the school program incorporates sign language as part of its methods of instruction. This should raise several important questions in your mind, such as:

1. If I am the greatest influence upon my child's language development, should I provide more input with respect to this decision?

2. Am I assuming that the educators are better prepared to make these decisions than I am?

3. If I wait until the educators make this decision for me, will a number of years pass before my child is exposed to language in an appropriate fashion?

4. If a child with normal hearing effortlessly learns language through immediate family contacts, should my hearing-impaired youngster be denied the same opportunity?

5. If my child spends more time with immediate family members during the early formative years, in spite of early intervention educational programs, is it possible that the family could prove far more influential regarding my child's language development?

6. If I select a communication system for my child soon after the hearing impairment is discovered, will my child suffer worse consequences had I delayed the decision?

7. Am I prepared to make a decision of this nature; and, if not, how can I better prepare myself to do so beyond evidence gathered through daily contacts with my child?

8. If normally hearing youngsters develop nearly 75 percent of their English grammar and syntax by the time they reach school age, shouldn't I assume that somewhat the same will occur in the case of my hearing-impaired child if the proper communication system is implemented at home?

9. If I wish to be supportive of my child's educational program and I want my child's schooling to support my efforts, isn't much of this responsibility mine?

You are your child's first and most intimate contact. Therefore, you can be the most influential and productive individuals regarding your youngster's language development.

SPEECH INTELLIGIBILITY

Speech development among the hearing-impaired is probably one of the most controversial issues debated by their parents, educators, researchers, and other related professionals. Unfortunately, few conclusions are reached on the basis of research, but rather on emotion or personal wishes. Differences of opinion have arisen and dwelled upon methods of communication, rather than the central issue—language development.

Although speech is the initial and most commonly-accepted form of language usage between two or more individuals, it is not necessarily the only method of thought communication. Granted, the absence of speech limits someone who attempts to function in a society that uses it as its principal mode of communication. This is a fact that hardly anyone would deny. But, to further restrict an individual for the sake of a method seems inadvisable, to say the least. In the absence of adequate research, you will need to make decisions regarding your child's communication system based upon realistic goals. Perhaps the following figures will provide you with some idea of what a sample population is accomplishing in terms of speech intelligibility. Remember, however, many variables determine someone's success in this respect. Your youngster's success will be determined through a combination of actual experience, the effect of variables, and the effort exerted by you and others involved with your child's development.

A study conducted by the Office of Demographic Studies in 1983 revealed that 55 percent of the sample population did not have intelligible speech while 45 percent did. Variables that affected this mix are shown in Figure 16-6.

**FREQUENCY CORRESPONDING TO FACTORS
AFFECTING SPEECH INTELLIGIBILITY**

Relationship	Speech Intelligibility	
	Not Intelligible	Intelligible
Total sample	54.7%	45.3%
Degree of hearing loss		
Less-than-severe	13.9%	86.1%
Severe	41.0%	59.0%
Profound	75.3%	24.7%
Student Communication method		
Speaks only	9.6%	90.4%
Signs only	93.1%	6.9%
Speaks and signs	59.8%	40.2%
Academic integration with hearing students		
None	68.9%	31.1%
Some	35.4%	64.6%
Additional handicapping conditions		
None	52.7%	47.3%
One or more	60.9%	39.1%

Figure 16.6. Figures used by permission of the publisher, College-Hill Press, San Diego, California 92105. *Deaf Children in America*, Edited by Arthur Schildroth and Michael Karchmer. Copyright 1984. Rights Reserved.

ACADEMIC ACHIEVEMENT

One of the more effective ways to determine whether your child is making satisfactory progress is through standardized tests. The most commonly used for hearing-impaired children is the Stanford Achievement Test—Hearing Impaired Norms. Although the battery has a number of subtests, they are basically a language evaluation, with the exception of mathematics computation which does not require reading comprehension to answer the problems. Therefore, most of the data reported in the literature is based upon these two subtest results.

Also, the plotting of these grade levels is based on a mean or average for each age level. This means that your child may fall close to, somewhat above, or below the mean grade level. Reading comprehension, of course, will give you some idea of where your child stands in comparison with a normally hearing population at the same age level (See Figs. 16.7 & 16.8). These mean grade levels indicate that:

1. The hearing-impaired fall well below normally hearing children in terms of reading comprehension and mathematics computation.
2. It seems as though the hearing-impaired population levels off at about third grade in reading comprehension and seventh grade in mathematics computation.

You should be aware that the children included in this survey were those who were receiving special education services throughout the United States. Those children with lesser hearing losses who did not require special education services were not included.

The Office of Demographic Studies indicated that there was a difference in reading comprehension between youngsters who were mainstreamed and those who attended special schools for the hearing-impaired. Although the grade level differences were slightly greater up to age fourteen, both groups levelled off thereafter with a one-half grade level difference in favor of those children who were mainstreamed. This, of course, is not nearly as great as the difference between the hearing-impaired population of either category and normally hearing children (See Fig. 16.9).

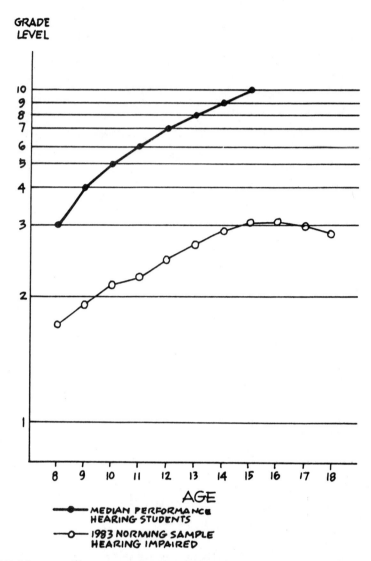

Figure 16.7. Mean reading comprehension by grade levels between hearing impaired and normally hearing children by age. Figures used by permission of the publisher, College-Hill Press, San Diego, California 92105. *Deaf Children In America,* Edited by Arthur Schildroth and Michael Karchmer. Copyright 1984. Rights Reserved.

SUMMARY

This chapter was designed to provide you with a more realistic view of the hearing-impaired population with respect to their distribution based

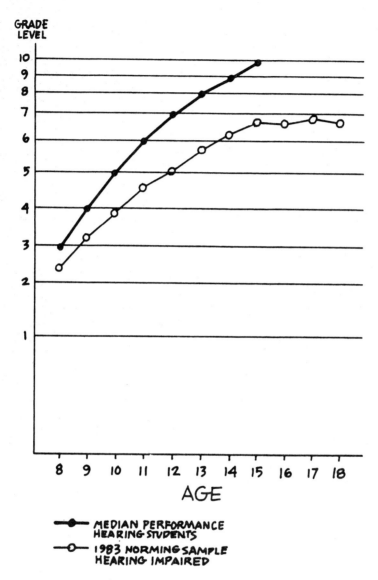

Figure 16.8. Mean mathematics computation grade levels as a function of age level. Figures used by permission of the publisher, College-Hill Press, San Diego, California 92105. *Deaf Children In America*, Edited by Arthur Schildroth and Michael Karchmer. Copyright 1984. Rights Reserved.

upon degree of hearing loss, the causes of hearing impairments, the distribution of youngsters who have more than one handicap, what types of schools these youngsters are attending, the types of communica-

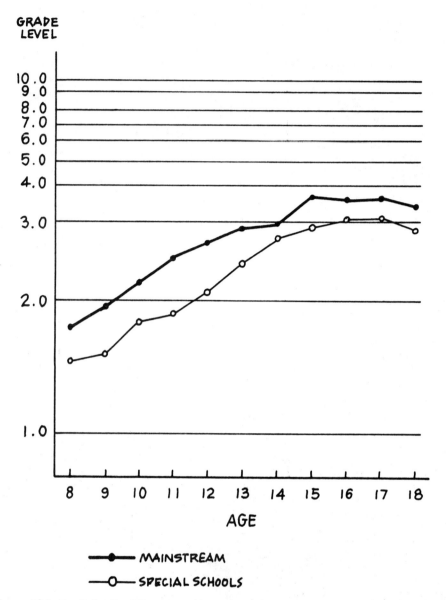

Figure 16.9. Grade level achievement scores as a function of age based on mainstreamed students vs special schools for the hearing impaired. Figures used by permission of the publisher, College-Hill Press, San Diego, California 92105. *Deaf Children In America*, Edited by Arthur Schildroth and Michael Karchmer. Copyright 1984. Rights Reserved.

tion systems employed, speech intelligibility, and average achievement levels.

You should be reminded that there is an absence of accurate research and measurement devices to determine where your child may stand in this spectrum of variables. Many of the statistics are based on an average drawn from large samples. However, your child's success will be determined on the basis of your efforts, the efforts of your child's educators, age of onset, degree of hearing loss, and ethnic background, to mention a few.

Chapter 17

DEVICES FOR THE HEARING IMPAIRED

INTRODUCTION

Even though your child wears a hearing aid, there are times when the instrument may not be in use or it may not adequately service your youngster. Therefore, you may wish to purchase one or more commercially-available items that will allow your child to communicate through vision or touch.

On the next several pages, you will find pictures of these items, with a brief description of each. If you wish to investigate these further, you should contact your audiologist or dispenser to determine where they can be obtained.

Many parents of hearing-impaired children assume that their child will be able to function adequately through the use of their hearing aid, or they are simply unaware of the availability of these items. The need for one or more of them will be self-evident, depending upon the extent of your child's hearing impairment.

SUMMARY

There are a variety of devices, other than a hearing aid, that you may find quite useful for your child's needs. This, of course, will depend largely upon the degree of your youngster's hearing impairment or the situation in which he finds himself. The presentation of these items is not intended to encourage you to purchase all of them, but to familiarize yourself with what is available. You or your child must determine which ones are useful.

155

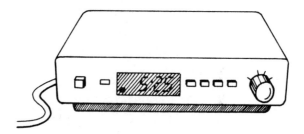

Figure 17.1. Digital alarm clock takes attachment for pillow vibrator or bed vibrator.

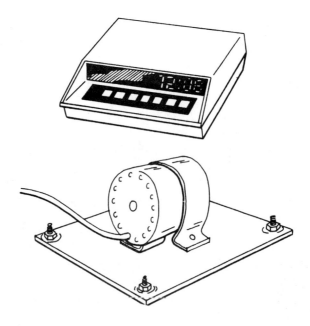

Figure 17.2. Heavy-duty timer with bed vibrator.

Figure 17.3. Telephone strobe light with loud horn alert.

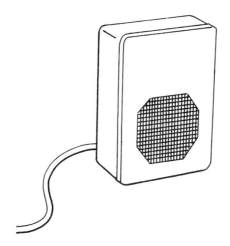

Figure 17.4. Horn alert for telephone or doorbell.

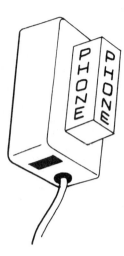

Figure 17.5. Strobe light phone alert for installation in any room.

Figure 17.6. Personal TV amplifier with volume control, stethascope headset or jack with stock, single mold.

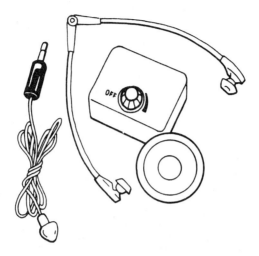

Figure 17.7. Doorbell horn activated each time the doorbell button is depressed.

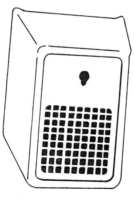

Figure 17.8. Baby or smoke alarm system activated by either source.

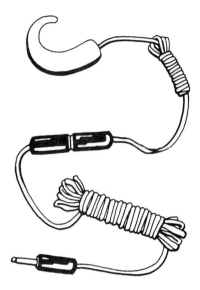

Figure 17.9. Accommodates to standard radio or television speaker system jacks with induction coil placement next to the hearing aid. The aid is placed on the T position and sound is transmitted through an electromagnetic field

Figure 17.10. Digital alarm clock radio with strobe light alert.

Figure 17.11. Strobe light attached to phone with strobe light alert.

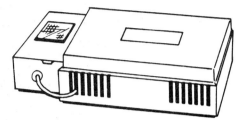

Figure 17.12. Doorbell attachment that activates strobe light when bell is pressed.

Figure 17.13. When both parties have this system, typed messages are transmitted electronically and appear on a screen. These instruments are used when voice calls are inappropriate.

Figure 17.14. Telephone headset with wheel volume control to amplify voices received.

Figure 17.15. Telephone headset with volume control touch bar.

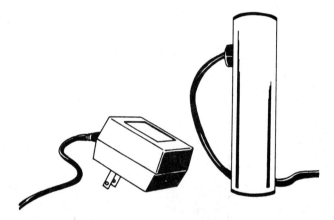

Figure 17.16. Vibrator attachment connected to clock timer/alarm system.

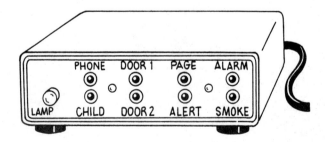

Figure 17.17. Receiver unit for a variety of alerting devices obtained separately.

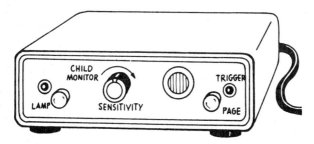

Figure 17.18. Monitor to be connected to central receiver which is activated by a child's cry or voice.

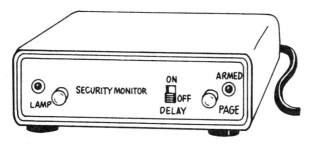

Figure 17.19. Monitor to be attached to central receiver to alert against illegal entry into the home.

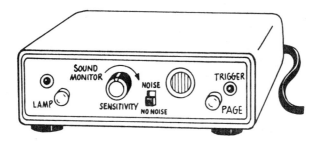

Figure 17.20. Monitor to be connected to central receiver responds to all types of noises.

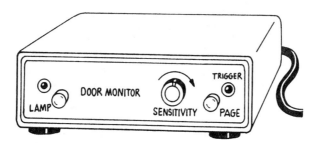

Figure 17.21. Monitor to be connected to central receiver and activated when doorbell rings.

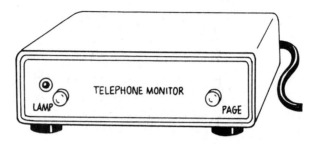

Figure 17.22. Monitor to be attached to central receiver is activated when the telephone rings.

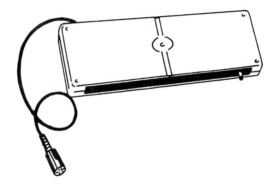

Figure 17.23. Television, radio or phonograph listening system. Picks up signal and transmits sound through infrared light.

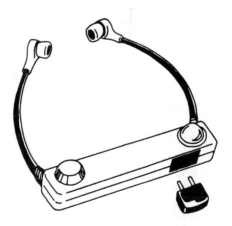

Figure 17.24. Receiver headset picks up signal through infrared light without the use of connecting wires.

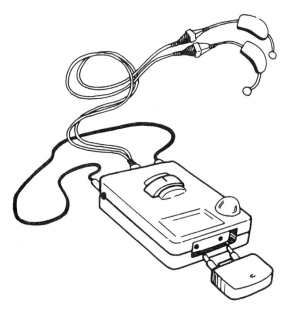

Figure 17.25. An infrared receiver designed to transport sound through tabs that are placed next to a behind-the-ear hearing aid. The aid(s) are placed on the T position, setting up an electromagnetic field, allowing amplification of the sound uninterrupted by separation of the hearing aid microphone and the speaker of the sound source.

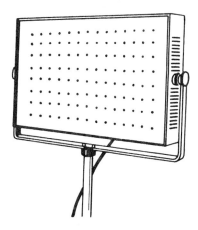

Figure 17.26. Infrared transmitter to be used in large theatres, meeting rooms or lecture halls.

Figure 17.27. The electronic transmission of messages through the use of a typewriter keyboard coupled with a telephone receiver. Messages appear on a screen and on a roll of paper when a permanent record is desired for future reference.

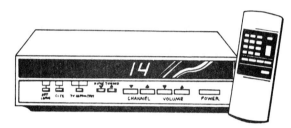

Figure 17.28. The decoder can be attached to a television set with the spoken word appearing in its printed form on the television screen.

Figure 17.29. Relay box for attachment of monitoring systems located throughout the house. Conducts signal through the wiring system to the receiver.

GLOSSARY

acoustic reflex thresholds —determines how well the stapedius muscle is working.

air-conducted sound —sounds that travel through the Outer, Middle, and Inner ear.

alveola —gum ridge covering teeth.

amplifier —increases the loudness of sound.

Amslan —the American Sign Language.

anatomy —structure.

articulators —the parts of the human anatomy that produce different speech sounds.

audiogram —a chart that contains the audiologist's test results.

aural —hearing.

binaural —two ears.

bone-conducted sounds —sounds that bypass the Outer and Middle ear by passing directly through the skull bones to the Inner Ear.

bone conduction —sound transmitted through the skull structure directly to the Inner Ear.

brain stem —main branch of the brain.

cerebral cortex —centers of the brain.

cerumen —wax.

cholesteatoma —tissue growth in the Middle Ear causing a false tumor.

cilia —nerve endings of hearing.

cochlea —snail-like structure of the Inner Ear containing the nerve endings of hearing.

cochlear implant —a method of amplification that inserts an electrical probe into the Inner Ear mechanism.

conductive —sound that is transmitted through the parts of Outer and Middle Ear.

congenital —dating from birth or acquired during development before birth.

167

consonant —a speech sound, voiced or unvoiced, that conforms or harmonizes with other sounds.

cued speech —combining speech with hand shapes and positions representing several consonant or vowel sounds.

decibel —a scale devised to measure loudness.

demographics —the statistical study of populations.

dentil — teeth.

diphthongs —a glide from one vowel sound to another.

due process —lawful procedures.

VIII cranial nerve —bundle of nerves leading to the brain stem at the center of hearing.

electrical energy —when sound waves activate the hair cells.

electrocardiogram —measures the rate of heartbeat.

electrocochleography —measures the stimulations of the nerve fibers of the Inner Ear.

electrodermal response —when a mild electric shock is given, the sweat glands of the skin change, varying the resistance.

etiology —causes.

Eustachian tube —a tube extending from the back of the throat to the Middle Ear cavity.

external auditory meatus —ear canal.

external otitis —bacteria or fungi causing infection of the ear canal.

fingerspelling —twenty-six hand configurations representing the letters of the alphabet.

formant —pitches to which a chamber or cavity is most responsive; e.g., vocal tract.

frequency —pitch. The number of times a tone repeats itself in a given period of time.

fundamental formant —lowest resonant frequency of a speech sound with the greatest loudness.

gain —the degree of loudness that a hearing aid will permit.

glottal —vocal tract.

grammar —a set of rules that governs the arrangement of words into sentences.

harmonics —whole-number multiples of fundamental formants.

homophenous —speech sounds that look alike on the lips but sound different.

hydraulic energy —sound waves passing through the fluids of the Inner Ear.

I.Q. —intelligence quotient.

impedance —the resistance to the flow of anything.

incus —the middle of the three bones of the Middle Ear.

labial —lips

labio-dental —lips and teeth.

Least Restrictive Environment (LRE) —that educational environment that provides a handicapped child with appropriate services to meet his or her needs.

malleus —Middle Ear bone closest to the eardrum.

manual communication —any form of language communication that is other than speech, reading, or writing words.

mastoid —bone structure surrounding the ear.

maximum power output —a limiting device in the hearing aid to prevent sound from causing discomfort or damage to the ear.

mechanical energy —sound traveling through the bones of the Middle Ear.

microphone —receives airborne sound and converts it to electrical impulses.

mixed type loss —a combination of conductive and sensorineural hearing impairment.

monaural —one ear.

morphology —how words change their form depending upon their use in a sentence.

mucous otitis media —when the fluid of the Inner Ear thickens.

myringotamy —surgical incision in the eardrum to allow for drainage of fluids from the Middle Ear or equalize air pressure on both sides of the eardrum.

neurological —dealing with the nervous system.

non-supperative —otitis media without the presence of fluid accumulation.

oscillator —an object that vibrates.

ossicles —three small bones located in the Middle Ear cavity.

otic cavity —Middle Ear cavity.

otitis media —inflammation or infection of the Middle Ear cavity.

otological —pertaining to the ear.

otologist —a physician who specializes in the treatment of the ears.

otosclerosis —a spongy bone-like growth that develops around the Middle Ear cavity.

palate — roof of the mouth.

percentile rank — a measure of how much an individual falls above or below an average point.

phonetically balanced word lists — the sounds of the language appear in the lists at a frequency that could be found when speaking in connected language.

physiology — function.

pinna — external shell-like structure of the ear.

pure oral — using speech only as a method of communication.

pure tone — a tone containing a single frequency.

receiver — converts an electronic sound to an airborne sound.

semantics — meaning of a sentence.

semicircular canals — part of the Inner Ear that accounts for balance and orientation in space.

sensorineural — sound that is transmitted through the Inner Ear hair-like cells to the brain.

serous otitis media — otitis media with the presence of a thin fluid.

Siglish — signed English.

sign language — hand and arm positions representing whole words.

simultaneous approach — using signs and finger spelling to approximate the word order of Standard English.

speech reception threshold — the minimum level of loudness necessary for an individual to barely hear and understand speech.

spondee — when the stress is placed equally on a two-syllable word.

standard deviation — a measure of how far one falls above or below an average point.

stapedectomy — surgically removed stapes bone of the Middle Ear.

stapes — the Inner Ear bone closest to the Inner Ear.

static compliance — determines whether the Middle Ear bones are moving properly.

surrogate — someone appointed to act in behalf of another individual, as in the case of a surrogate parent.

syntax — word order.

temporal lobe — the portion of the brain where sounds are interpreted and understood.

threshold — the point of loudness at which one is just barely able to detect a sound.

total communication — a philosophy that supports the use of all methods of communication, depending upon an individual's particular need.

tympanic membrane —eardrum.

tympanometry —a variance in air pressure in the ear canal to determine the air pressure inside the eardrum.

velum —solf palate at the back of the mouth's roof.

vibro-tactile —feeling speech vibrations.

vowel —a voiced speech sound that does not block the speech channel.

BIBLIOGRAPHY

Aldridge, L.D.: Family Learning Vacation: An Implementation Guide, Special School of the Future, Gallaudet College, Washington, D.C., 1980.

Allen, T., Osborn, T.: Academic Integration of Hearing Impaired Students: Demographic, Handicapping and Achievement Factors, A.A.D., 1980.

Ayer, H.: *Auditory Perception in Auditory Communication for the Hard of Hearing.* Prentice-Hall, Englewood Cliffs, 1966.

Baker, B.L.: Parent involvement in programming for developmentally disabled children. In Lloyd, L.L. (Ed.): *Communication Assessment and and Intervention Strategies,* pp. 691–733. University Park Press, Baltimore, 1976.

Bess, F.H. (Ed.): *Childhood Deafness: Causation, Assessment, and Management.* Grune and Stratton, New York, 1977.

Blanco, R.: *Prescriptions for Children with Learning and Adjustment Problems,* 2d ed., Thomas, Springfield, 1982.

Brill, R.G.: *Mainstreaming the Prelingually Deaf Child.* Gallaudet College Press, Washington, D.C.

Brill, R.G., Merrill, E., Jr., and Frisina, D.R.: Recommended Organizational Policies in the Education of the Deaf. Conference of Executives of American Schools for the Deaf. Washington, D.C., 1973.

Brutton, M., Manuel, G.: *Something Wrong With My Child.* Harcourt, Brace Jovanovich, New York, 1973.

Catlin, F.I.: Etiology and pathology of hearing loss in children. In Martin, F.N. (Ed.): *Pediatric Audiology,* pp. 3–34. Prentice-Hall, Englewood Cliffs, 1978.

Chasin, W.D.: The clinical management of otologic disorders. In Bradford, L.J., and Hardy, W.G. (Eds.): *Hearing and Hearing Impairment,* pp. 93–108. Grune and Stratton, New York, 1979.

Chess, S., Fernandez, P., and Korn, S.: The handicapped child and his family: Consonance and dissonance, with special reference to deaf children. Journal of the American Academy of Child Psychiatry, *19:*56–57.

Clarke, B.R., and Ling, D.: The effects of using cued speech: A follow-up study. Volta Review *78(1):*23–34.

Colin, C.: *On Human Communication.* Wiley, New York, 1957.

Council for Exceptional Children. Resolution: Least Restrictive Environment and Quality Educational Program for Exceptional Children (passed unanimously at April Delegate Assembly). CED, Reston, Virginia, 1980.

Craig, W.N.: Effects of preschool training on the Development of reading and lipreading skills of deaf children. American Annals of the Deaf, *199:*280–296, 1964.

Dale, D.: *Language Development in Deaf and Partially Hearing Children.* Springfield, Thomas, 1974.

Dale, P.S.: *Language Development: Structure and Function.* 2nd ed. Holt, Rinehart and Winston, New York, 1976.

Davis, H.: *Hearing and Deafness.* Holt, Rinehart and Winston, New York. Rev. Ed., 1965.

Denes, P., and Pinson, E.: *The Speech Chain.* Bell Telephone Labs., 1963.

Doerfler, L.: How we hear and how noise affects our hearing. National Safety News, July, 143, 1956.

Donnelly, K., et al.: *Interpreting Hearing Aid Technology.* Springfield, Thomas, 1974.

Fairchild, B.: Parental concerns. Journal of Rehabilitation of the Deaf, *12:*84–90.

Faunt, G.: *Acoustic Theory of Speech Production.* Moreton, 1960.

Fletcher, H.: *Speech and Hearing in Communication.* Van Nostrand, New York, 1953.

Freeman, R.D., Malkin, S.F., and Hastings, J.O.: Psychosocial problems of deaf children and their families: A comparative study. American Annals of the Deaf, *120:*391–405.

Friedman, M.: The Changing Profile of the Labor Force. AFL–CIO American Federalist *74:*7–14, 1967.

Fulton, R., and Lloyd, L., et al.: *Audiometry for the Retarded,* Williams and Wilkins, Baltimore, 1969.

Furth, H.G.: *Thinking Without Language: Psychological Implications of Deafness.* Free Press, New York/Collier-Macmillan, London, 1966.

Furth, H.G.: *Deafness and Learning: A Psychosocial Approach.* Wadsworth, Belmont, California, 1973.

Goldberg, S., and Deutsch, F.: *Life Span: Individual and Family Development.* Brooks/Cole, Belmont, California, 1977.

Greenberg, J.: *In This Sign.* Holt, Rinehart, and Winston, New York, 1970.

Greenberg, M.: Hearing families with deaf children: Stress and functioning as related to communication method. American Annals of the Deaf, *125:*1063–1071, 1980a.

Greenberg, M.: Mode use in deaf children: The effects of communication method and communication competence. Applied Psycholinguistics *1:*65–79, 1980b.

Gregory, S.: *The Deaf Child and His Family.* Halsted, New York, Allen and Unwin, London, 1976.

Hirsh, I.J.: *The Measurement of Hearing.* McGraw-Hill, New York, 1952.

International Association of Parents of the Deaf. Position Statements (Focus on Education: Public Law 94-142; Least Restrictive Environment; Child Evaluation and Placement; Individualized Education Program; Characteristics of an Appropriate Educational Program; Mainstreaming; Due Process). IAPD, Silver Spring, Maryland, 1979.

Jerger, J., et al.: *Handbook of Clinical Impedance Audiometry.* American Electromedics Corporation, 1975.

Jerger, J.: *Modern Developments in Audiology.* Academic Press, San Diego, 1963.

Jones, D.: *An Outline of English Phonetics.* W. Hefner & Sons, 1956.

Kaplan, H.M.: *Anatomy and Physiology of Speech.* McGraw-Hill, New York, 1960.

Karchmer, M.A., Milone, M.N., Jr. and Wolk, S.: Educational significance of hearing loss at three levels of severity. American Annals of the Deaf, *124:*97–109.

Karnes, M.B.: *Learning Language at Home, No. 2.* The Council for Exceptional Children, 1978.

Katz, J.: *Handbook of Clinical Audiology.* Williams and Wilkins, Baltimore, 1972.

Katz, L., Mathis, S.L. III, and Merrill, E.C., Jr.: *The Deaf Child in the Public Schools: A Handbook for Parents of Deaf Children.* 2nd ed. Interstate, Danville, Illinois, 1978.

Levine, E.: *The Psychology of Deafness.* Columbia University Press, New York, 1960.

Ling, D.: Auditory coding and recoding: An analysis of auditory training procedures for hearing-impaired children. In Ross, M. and Giolas, T.G. (Eds.): *Auditory Management of Hearing-Impaired Children: Principles and Prerequisites for Intervention,* pp. 181–218. University Park Press, Baltimore, 1978.

Ling, D. and Ling, A.: Aural Habilitation: The Foundations of Verbal Learning in Hearing-Impaired Children. The A.G. Bell Association, Washington, D.C., 1978.

Lloyd, L.I., and Kaplan, H.: *Audiometric Interpretation: A Manual of Basic Audiometry.* University Park Press, Baltimore, 1978.

Meadow, K.P., and Trybus, R.J.: Behavioral and emotional problems of deaf children: An overview. In Bradford, J.J. and Hardy, W.G. (Eds.): *Hearing and Hearing Impairment,* pp. 395–403. Grune and Stratton, New York, 1979.

Miller, G.A.: *Language and Communication.* McGraw-Hill, New York, 1951.

Miller, J.B.: *Oralism.* Volta Review, *72:*211–17, 1970.

Mindel, E.D.: A Child Psychiatrist Looks at Deafness, Deaf American, *20:*15–19, 1968.

Mindel, E.D., and McCoy, V.: *They Grow in Silence: The Deaf Child and His Family.* National Association of the Deaf, 1971.

Moores, D.F.: Communication Psycholinguistics and Deafness: Proceedings of the Teachers Institute, Maryland School for the Deaf, 1969.

Moores, D.F., Weiss, K.L., and Goodwin, M.W.: Early education programs for hearing impaired children: Major findings. American Annals of the Deaf, *123:*925–936.

Moskowitz, B.A.: The acquisition of language. Scientific American, *239(5):*92–108.

Myklehurst, H.: *Auditory Disorders in Children.* Grune and Stratton, New York, 1954.

Naiman, D. and Schein, J.D.: *For Parents of Deaf Children.* National Association of the Deaf, Silver Spring, Maryland, 1978.

Newby, H.A.: *Audiology,* 2nd ed. Appleton-Century-Crafts, 1964.

Northern, J.L., and Downs, M.: *Hearing in Children.* Williams and Wilkins, Baltimore, 1974.

Palmer, J.O.: *The Psychological Assessment of Children.* Wiley, New York, 1970.

Phillips, W.D.: Influence of Preschool Training on Achievement in Language Arts, Arithmetic Concepts and Socialization of Young Deaf Children. Doctoral diss., Teachers College, Columbia University, 1963.

Public Law 94-142, Education For All Handicapped Children Act, November 29, 1975.

Quigley, S.P.: The Influence of Finger Spelling on the Development of Language, Communication and Educational Achievement in Deaf Children. Department of Special Education, University of Illinois, Urbana, Illinois, 1968.

Reilly, J., and McIntire, M.L.: American Sign Language and Pidgin Sign English: What's the difference? Sign Language Studies, *27:*151–192.

Rose, D.E., and Shearer, W.M.: Cortical Audiometry for Children. E.E.N.T. Digest, *30:*61–64, 1968.

Ross, M.: Hearing aids. In Jaffe, B.F. (Ed.): *Hearing Loss in Children,* pp. 676–698, University Park Press, Baltimore, 1977.

Ross, M., and Giolas, T.G. (Eds.): *Auditory Management of Hearing-Impaired Children: Principles and Prerequisites for Intervention.* University Park Press, Baltimore, 1978.

Schein, J.D., and Bushaq, S.: Higher Education for the Deaf in the United States. American Annals of the Deaf, 107:416–20, 1962.

Schildroth, A.N., and Karchner, M.A.: *Deaf Children in America.* College Hill Press, 1986.

Schlesinger, H.: Prevention, diagnosis, and habilitation of deafness: A critical look. In Hicks, D. (Ed.): Medical Aspects of Deafness (National Forum No. 4), pp. 19–30. Council of Organizations Serving the Deaf, Washington, D.C. 1971.

Schlesinger, H.: Diagnostic crises. In Culton, P.M. (Ed.): *Operation Tripod: Toward Rehabilitation Involvement by Parents of the Deaf,* pp. 20–25. Pub. no. SRS 74-25020, U.S. Government Printing Office, Washington, D.C., 1974.

Schlesinger, H.S., and Meadow, K.P.: *Sound and Sign: Childhood Deafness and Mental Health.* University of California Press, Berkeley, 1972.

Sonotone Corporation: *Educating Your Hearing.* Sonotone, 1941.

Sonotone Corporation: *How to Improve Your Speech.* Sonotone, 1941.

Sonotone Corporation: *Introduction to Lipreading.* Sonotone, 1941.

Staab, W.J.: *Hearing Aid Handbook.* Tab Books, 2nd ed., 1978.

Stokoe, W.C.: *Sign Language Structure: The First Linguistic Analysis of American Sign Language* (revised edition). Linstok Press, Silver Spring, Maryland, 1978.

Tracy, Spencer et al.: *If You Have a Deaf Child.* University of Illinois Press, Champaign, 1965.

Trybus, R., and Karchner, M.: *The Demographics of Deafness Resulting from Maternal Rubella.* A.A.D., 1980.

VanBergeijk, W.A., Pierce, J.R., and David, E.: *Waves and the Ear.* Anchor Books, Doubleday and Company, Garden City, New York, 1960.

Van Riper, C.: *Speech Correction—Principles and Methods,* 4th ed., 1964.

Vernon, M.: Fifty years of research on the intelligence of deaf and hard of hearing children: A review of literature and discussions. Journal of Rehabilitation of the Deaf, *1:*4–7, 1968.

Vernon, M.: Multiply Handicapped Deaf Children: Medical, Educational, and Psychological Aspects. Council of Exceptional Children, 1969.

Vernon, M.: The Relationships of Language to the Thinking Process. Archives of General Psychiatry, 16:325–33, 1967.

Vernon, M., and Koh, S.D.: Effects of early manual communication on achievement of deaf children. American Annals of the Deaf, *115:*527–536, 1970.

Vernon, M., and Kohn, S.D.: Effects of oral preschool compared to early manual communication on education and communication in deaf children. American Annals of the Deaf, *116:*569–574.

Victoreen, J.: *Hearing Enhancement.* Thomas, Springfield, 1960.

Walk, S., Allen, T.: A five-year follow up of reading comprehension achievement of hearing-impaired students in special education programs. The Journal of Special Education, Vol. 18, No. 2, 1984.

Whatmough, J.: *Language.* St. Martin's Press, 1957.

Williams, B.R., and Vernon, M.: *Vocational Guidance: On Hearing and Deafness.* 3rd ed. Holt, Rinehart and Winston, New York, 1970.

Yanick, P.: *You Can Hear Better,* 2nd ed. Sunshine Press, West Palm Beach, 1984.

Zemlin, W.R.: *Speech and Hearing Science.* Prentice-Hall, New York, 1968.

INDEX

A

Academic achievement, 149–153
  use Stanford Achievement Test (*see*
    Stanford Achievement Test)
Acoustic reflex thresholds, 47
  definition, 167
Air-conducted sound, 18, 21
  definition, 167
  skull bone movement, diagram, 20
  transmission of, diagram, 19
Aldridge, L. D., 173
Alerting devices
  monitors, illustrations, 163, 164
  receiver unit, illustration, 162
Allen, T., 173, 177
Alveola, definition, 167
American School for the Deaf, 132
Amplifier, definition, 167
Amslan
  definition, 167
  use of, 98
    illustrations, 99
Anatomy, definition, 167
Articulators, definition, 167
Audiogram, definition, 36, 167
Audiological evaluations, 35–50
  considerations in, 36
  degrees of hearing loss, 37–38
    audiogram, 37
  hearing aid evaluation, 49–50
  objective tests, 45–49
    electrocochleography, 49
    electrodermal response audiometry,
      47–49
    electroencephalographic evoked-
      response, audiometry, 49
    heart-rate response audiometry,
      49
    impedance audiometry, 47

role of audiologist, 35
subjective tests, 36–41
  pure tone audiometry (*see*
    Pure tone audiometry)
summary, 50
testing children aged two to five years,
  42, 45
  audiological test results, 43, 44, 46
  testing children five to eighteen years,
    45
  testing infants of up to 24 months,
    41–42
  types testing by age, 41
Audiologist, role of, 35
Auditory training, 107–108
Aural, definition, 167
Ayer, H., 173

B

Baby alarm device, illustration, 159
  monitor, illustration, 163
Baker, B. L., 173
Balla, David A., 77
Behavior management hearing impaired
  child, 11–12
Behind-the-ear hearing aid, 52
  diagram, 53
Bell, Alexander Graham, 132
Bell, A. Melville, 132
Bess, F. H., 173
Bevan, Frances, xi
Bevan, Ruth, xii
Bevan, Warren, xii
Biaural, definition, 167
Blanco, R., 173
Bochrach, Albert, xi
Bone conduction, definition,
  167

Bone-conducted sounds, 18–21
    definition, 19, 167
    transmission of, diagram, 19
Bradford, J. J., 175
Bradford, L. J., 173
Braidwood, Thomas, 132
Brain stem, definition, 167
Brill, R. G., 173
Brutton, M., 173
Burglar alarm device, monitor for, 163
Bushaq, S., 176

C

Catlin, F. I., 173
Central deafness, 33–34
    causes of, 33–34
    treatment, 34
Cerebral cortex, definition, 167
Cerumen, definition, 167
Chasin, W. D., 173
Chess, S., 173
Cholesteatoma
    definition, 167
    hearing impairment due to, 29
    treatment, 29
Cicchetti, Domenic, 77
Cilia
    definition, 167
    diagram, 16
Clarke, B. R., 173
Cochlea
    definition, 167
    diagram, 16, 17, 18
Cochlear implant
    criteria candidates for, 52
    definition, 167
    procedure, diagram, 55
Colin, C., 173
Communication and hearing impaired child
    emotional impact of, 10
    importance effective system, 9
    social impact of, 10
    total family involvement in process,
        10–11
Communication systems, 95–101
    Amslan (American Sign Language), 98
        illustrations, 99
    cued speech, 99

illustration, 101
    fingerspelling (Rochester method), 97
        alphabet illustrated, 97
    goals of, 103–104
    manual communication, 108–110
        advantages, 109–110
        selection of method, 109
    methods of communicating, 103–104
    pure oral method, 96
    selection of, 95–96
    siglish (signed English), 97–98
        illustrations, 98
    simultaneous approach, 99
        illustrations, 100
    speech (*see* Speech)
    speechreading (*see* Speechreading)
    summary, 101
    total communication, 100–101
    use of, survey results, 145–147
        factors in, 146–147
Conductive type hearing loss
    definition, 23, 167
    etiology and treatment
        cerumen, 24
        cholesteatoma, 29
        congenital malformation, 24
        external otitis, 24
        otosclerosis, 30–31
Congenital, definition, 167
Consonant, definition, 168
Cozzolino, Sandy, xi
Craig, W. N., 173
Cranial nerve, eighth (*see*
        Eighth cranial nerve)
Cued speech
    definition, 168
    use of, 99
        illustration, 101
Culton, P. M., 176

D

Dale, D., 174
Dale, P. S., 174
David, E., 176
Davis, H., 174
Day schools, 120–121
Decibel, definition, 168
de l'Epee, Abbe Charles Michel, 132

Delgade Junior College, New Orleans,
    Louisiana, 133
Demographics, 141–166
    academic achievement, 149–153
    communication systems (*see*
        Communication systems)
    definition, 168
    hearing impaired population data (*see*
        Hearing impaired)
    multiply handicapped, 144–145
    parental concerns, 141
    source of data, 141
    speech intelligibility, 147–148
Denes, P., 174
Dentil, definition, 168
Deutsch, F., 174
Devices for hearing impaired persons
    illustrations, 156–166
        baby or smoke alarm, 159
        digital alarm clock, 156, 160
        doorbell attachment, 157, 159, 161
        for telephone, 157, 158, 160, 161, 162
        infrared receiver to hearing aid, 165
        infrared transmitter for large rooms,
            165
        monitors, 163, 164
        personal TV amplifier, 158
        phonograph listening device, 164
        radio listening device, 164
        radio or television speaker system
            jacks, 160
        receiver headset, 164
        relay box for monitoring system, 166
        television listening device, 164
        television set decoder, 166
        timer with bed vibrator, 156
        typed message system, 161
        typewriter electronic message
            transmitter, 166
        vibrator attachment to clock timer/alarm
            system, 162
Digital alarm clock for hearing impaired,
    illustrations
    for pillow or bed vibrator, 156
    timer with bed vibrator, 156
    vibrator attachment for, 162
    with strobe light alert, 160
Diphthongs, definition, 168
Doerfler, L., 174

Donnelly, K., 174
Doorbell for hearing impaired, illustrations
    horn activated when button depressed, 159
    horn alert, 157
    monitor for, illustration, 163
    with strobe light, 161
Downs, M., 175

E

Ear
    anatomy of, 15–16
        sectional diagram, 16, 17
        structure, 15–16
    inner ear
        diagram, 16, 17, 18
        structure, 15–16
    middle ear
        diagram, 16, 17, 18
        structure, 15
    outer ear
        diagram, 16, 17, 18
        structure, 15
    physiology, 17–21
        air-conducted sound, 17
        bone-conducted sounds, 17–21
    sectional diagram, 16, 18
    semicircular canals structure, 16
Ear canal (*see* External auditory
    meatus)
Eardrum (*see* Otic cavity)
Education for all Handicapped Children Act
    (P.L. 94–142, 113
    architectural barriers, 118
    assurance nondiscriminatory testing &
        evaluation, 116
    assurance of extensive child identification
        procedures, 114
    assurance for surrogate to act for child, 117
    assurance of "full services" goals &
        detailed timetable, 114
    assurance of regular parent/guardian
        consultations, 115
    assurance of special education in least
        restrictive environment, 116–117
    guarantee of complete due process
        procedures, 114–115
    guarantees of policies & procedures to
        protect data confidentiality, 116

Education for all Handicapped Children Act
(*continued*)
  in-service training, 117
  maintenance of an I.E.P., 117
  options (*see* Educational options)
  right to a free education, 113
Educational options, 119–122
  parent role, 121–122
  programs, 119–121
    day school, 120–121
    home bound instruction, 122
    mainstreaming with supportive
      services, 120
    residential schools, 121
    resource room, 120
    total mainstreaming, 119
Educational programming, 12
Eighth cranial nerve
  definition, 168
  diagram, 16, 17, 18
Electrical energy
  definition, 18, 168
  diagram, 19
Electrocardiogram, definition, 168
Electrocochleography, 49
  definition, 168
Electrodermal response, definition, 168
Electrodermal response audiometry, 47–49
Electroencephalographic evoked-response
  audiometry, 49
Etiology, definition, 168
Eustachian tube
  definition, 168
  diagram, 16, 12, 18
External auditory meatus
  definition, 168
  diagram, 16
External otitis
  definition, 168
    treatment of, 24
Eyeglass hearing aid, 52
  diagram, 55

F

Fairchild, B., 174
Family of hearing impaired child, 7–12
  acceptance hearing impaired child
    by extended family, 9
    by parents, 8
    by sibling, 8–9
  activities at home, 13
  behavior management by, 11–12
  communication system (*see* Communication
    system)
  description of, 7
  educational programming, 12
  extended, 7
  mother's acceptance of child, 11
  nuclear, 7
  out-of-school activities, 12–13
  summary, 13
Faunt, G., 174
Fernandez, P., 173
Fingerspelling (Rochester method)
  alphabet illustrated, 97
  definition, 168
  use of, 97
Fletcher, H., 174
Formant
  definition, 168
  fundamental, defined, 168
Freeman, R. D., 174
Frequency, definition, 168
Friedman, M., 174
Frisina, D. Robert, viii, xi, 173
Fulton, R., 174
Fundamental formant, definition, 168
Furth, H. G., 174

G

Gain, definition, 168
Gallaudet, Thomas H., 132
Gallaudet College
  description, 133
  founding of, 132
Giolas, T. G., 175, 176
Glottal, definition, 168
Goldberg, S., 174
Goodwin, M. W., 175
Grammar, definition, 81, 168
Greenberg, J., 174
Greenberg, M., 174
Gregory, S., 174
Grieving process, 3–6
  acceptance stage, 5
  anger stage, 5

Grieving process (*continued*)
  bargaining stage, 4–5
  denial stage, 4
  guilt stage, 5
  summary, 6

H

Hardy, W. G., 173, 175
Harmonics, definition, 168
Hastings, J. D., 174
Hearing aid evaluation, 49–50
Hearing aids
  behind-the-ear, 52
    diagram, 53
  body style, 52, 53–54
    diagram, 54
  choice of, 56–57, 103
    character of aid, 57
    selection dispenser, 57
    selection which ear, 56–57
    type of, 56
  cochlear implant, 52
  components of, 51
    diagram, 52
  eyeglass, 52
    diagram, 55
  functions of, 54–57
    frequency, 56
    gain, 56
  in-the-ear, 52, 53
    diagram, 53
  performance of, 57–59
  summary, 59
  types of, 52–54
Hearing impairment
  ability of to understand speech,
    142–143
    table, 144
  devices for, 155 (*see also* Devices for
    hearing impaired)
    illustrations, 156–166
    summary, 155
  distribution of by age and sex,
    table, 142
  effect Vocational Rehabilitation Act
    on education of, 133–134
  etiology and medical treatment,
    23–24, 143–144

central deafness, 33–34
  conductive-type (*see* Conductive-
    type loss)
  mixed-type (*see* Mixed-type loss)
  sensorineural type (*see* Sensorineural
    type loss)
    table, 145
  first schools for the deaf, 132
  history of education for, 132
  language development, 104, 110
    considerations, 82–84
    importance of, 104
    methods used, 105
  nineteenth century education, 131–132
  number youths with in general population,
    142
  parental concerns, 141
  production speech in hearing impaired
    person, 82–84
    diagram, 83
    speechreading, 84
  production speech in normal hearing
    persons, 82–83
    diagram, 83
  program type, table, 143
  right to a free education, 113
  summary, 34
Heart-rate response audiometry, 49
Hicks, D., 176
Hirsh, I. J., 174
Hiskey-Nebraska Test of Learning Aptitude
    for Young Deaf Children, 66
    illustration, 67
Holmes, Emily, xi
Home bound instruction, 121
Homophenous, definition, 168
House-Tree-Person, 72–73
Human Figure Drawing, 72–73
Hydraulic energy, definition, 18, 169

I

Impedance, definition, 169
Impedance audiometry, 47
Incus, definition, 169
Individualized Educational Program (I.E.P.),
    123–130
  conferences, 124–125
    preplanning, 124

Individualized Educational Program (I.E.P.)
(*continued*)
    revision, 125
    contents of, 125–130
    face sheet of, 125
        sample, 126
    instructional areas of, 27, 130
        sample page, 129
    maintenance of, 117
    of P. L. 94–142, 112, 122
    preplanning conference, 124
    present education levels data, 125, 127
        form used illustrated, 128
    revision conference, 125
    right of parents, 123
    staff members involved, 124
    summary, 130
Intelligence testing, 64–66
    intelligence quotient, 64
        categories, 65
        deviation, 65
        distribution, 65
        formula for, 64
In-the-ear hearing aid, 52, 53
    diagram, 53
I.Q. (*see* Intelligence quotient)

J

Jaffe, B. F., 176
Jerger, J., 174
Jones, D., 175

K

Kaplan, H. M., 175
Karchmer, Michael A., 135, 136, 137, 138,
    139, 142, 143, 144, 145, 146, 148, 150,
    151, 152, 175, 176
Karnes, M. B., 175
Katz, J., 175
Katz, L., 175
Koh, S. D., 176
Kohn, S. D., 177
Korn, S., 173

L

Labial, definition, 169
Labio-dental, definition, 169

Language development, 81–84
    considerations for hearing impaired, 82–84
    developmental sequence, 82
    language defined, 81
    rules for, 81–82
    summary, 84
Least Restrictive Environment (LRE)
    definition, 169
    right to education in, 116–117
Legal aspects, 113–118
    Public Law 94–142 (*see* Education for
        All Handicapped Children Act)
    summary, 118
    Leiter International Performance Scale,
        66–67
        illustration, 68
    Levine, E., 175
    Ling, A., 175
    Ling, D., 173, 175
    Lipreading (*see* Speechreading)
    Lloyd, L. I., 175
    Lloyd, L. L., 173, 174

M

Mainstreaming
    total, 119
    with supportive services, 120
Malkin, S. F., 174
Malleus, definition, 169
Manual communication (*see also*
        Communication systems)
    definition, 169
Manuel, G., 173
Martin, F. N., 173
Mastoid, definition, 169
Mathis, S. L. III, 175
Maximum power output, definition, 169
McCoy, V., 175
McIntire, M. L., 176
Meadow, K. P., 175, 176
Mechanical energy
    definition, 18, 169
    diagram, 19
Merrill, E. C. Jr., 173, 175
Merrill-Palmer Scale of Mental Tests, 68–69
    illustration, 70
Message system for hearing impaired,
    illustrations

Message system for hearing impaired
(*continued*)
  with typewriter, 161, 166
Microphone, definition, 169
Miller, G. A., 175
Miller, J. B., 175
Milone, M. N. Jr., 175
Mindel, E. D., 175
Mixed type hearing loss, 33
  definition, 23, 169
Monoaural, definition, 169
Moores, D. F., 175
Morphology, definition, 82, 169
Moskowitz, B. A., 175
Mucous otitis media, definition, 169
Multiply handicapped
  prevalence of, 144–145
    graph, 146
Myklehurst, H., 175
Myringotomy, definition, 169

N

Naiman, D., 175
Marzisi, Lois, xi
National Technical Institute for the Deaf
    (NTID), 132–133
  description, 133
  foundation of, 132–133
Neurological, definition, 169
New York School for the Deaf, 132
Newby, H. A., 175
Noise alarm, monitor, illustration, 163
Nonsupperative, definition, 169
Northern, J. L., 175
Northridge, California, 133

O

Osborn, T., 173
Oscillator, definition, 169
Ossicles
  definition, 169
  diagram, 16, 18
Otic cavity
  definition, 169
  diagram, 16
Otitis media
  area of, diagram, 25

definition, 169
mucous, 26–28
  diagram, 30
  prevention, 28
  symptoms, 28
  treatment, 27
nonsupperative, 26
  diagrams, 26, 27
serous, 26
  diagram, 28
treatment of, 24–25
types of, 25–29
Otologist, definition, 169
Otosclerosis
  definition, 169
  hearing impairment due to, 30–31
  treatment of, 31
    diagram, 31, 32

P

Palate, definition, 170
Percentile rank, definition, 170
Phillips, W. D., 175
Phonetically balanced word lists,
    definition, 170
Physiology, definition, 170
Pinna, 15
  definition, 170
  illustration, 16
Pierce, J. R., 176
Pinson, E., 174
Postsecondary education, 131–140
  areas of study, 137–138
    career clusters, table, 138
    numbers of, graph, 139
  development of, 131
  effect Vocational Rehabilitation Act
    on, 133–134
  Gallaudet College, 132
  National Technical Institute for
    the Deaf, 132–133
  number programs, 134
    graph, 135
  Post-Secondary Educational
    Consortium, Univ. Tenn., 133
  regional programs for hearing-
    impaired, 133
  services offered, 134–135

Postsecondary education (*continued*)
  support services, table, 137
  summary, 138–140
  total enrollment hearing-impaired in
    college, 134
    graph, 136
Pure oral communication system, 96
  definition, 170
Pure tone audiometry, 36–45
  audiograms, 37, 38, 39
  definition, 170
  frequency, 37
  loudness, 36–37
  speech audiometry (*see* Speech audiometry)
Psychological evaluations, 63–80
  developmental evaluation, 72–73
    House-Tree-Person, 72–73
    Human Figure Drawing, 72–73
    parent conference, 73
    parent conference outline, illustration,
      78–80
    Vineland Adaptive Behavior Scale, 73
  intelligence testing, 64, 66
  psychologists' skills, 62–63
  purpose & types tests selected, 61–62
  setting for, 63–64
  summary, 74
  tests used, 66–69
    Hiskey-Nebraska Test of Learning
      Aptitude for Young Deaf
      Children, 66
    Leiter International Performance
      Scale, 66–67
    Merrill-Palmer Scale of Mental
      Tests, 68–69
    Stanford Binet Test of Intelligence, 69
    Wechsler Tests, 69

Q

Quigley, S. P., 176

R

Receiver, definition, 170
Radio speaker system for hearing aid,
  illustration, 160
Reilly, J., 176
Residential schools, 121

Resource room, 120
Rose, D. E., 176
Ross, M., 175, 176

S

St. Paul Technical Vocational Institute (TVI),
  St. Paul, Minnesota, 133
Schein, J. D., 175, 176
Schildroth, Arthur N., 135, 136, 137, 138, 139,
  142, 143, 144, 145, 146, 148, 150, 151, 152,
  176
Schlesinger, H. S., 176
Schrepfer, Kenneth, xi
Seattle Community College, Seattle,
  Washington, 133
Self-contained classes, 120
Semantics, definition, 82, 170
Semicircular canals
  definition, 170
  sectional diagram, 16, 18
Sensorineural hearing loss causes, 32–33
  definition, 23, 170
  treatment, 33
Serous otitis media, definition, 170
Shearer, W. M., 176
Siglish
  definition, 170
  use of, 97–98
    illustration, 98
Smoke alarm system, illustration, 159
Sign language, definition, 170
Simultaneous approach, definition, 170
Sound
  air-conducted, 18
  bone-conducted, 18–21
  transmission of, sectional diagram, 19
Sparks, Estelle, xi
Sparrow, Sara S., 77
Speech
  and hearing (*see* Speech and hearing)
  auditory training, 107–108
  in hearing-impaired, 104–105
  intelligibility of, 147–148
    factors affecting, table, 148
  manual communication, 108–110
  production of, 85–88
    consonants, 87
    diphthongs, 86–87

Speech (*continued*)
   formants, 88
   parts of body used, diagram, 86
   placement articulators, 87
   pure vowels, 85–86, 87
   voiced and unvoiced, 85–86
   production of in hearing-impaired
      persons, 82–84
   diagram, 83
   speechreading, 84
   production of in normal hearing
      persons, 82–83
   diagram, 83
   speechreading (*see* Speechreading)
   summary, 110–111
Speech and Hearing (*see also* Speech)
   duration of sound, 91
   formants, 88
    within hearing range, line graph, 89
   hearing speech, 91–92
   intensity average level, 88
    line graph, 90
   placement of articulators, 87
    definitions, 878
   presence/absence of sound, 91
   speaking, 92–93
    defective hearing feedback, diagram, 92
    normal feedback mechanism,
      diagram, 92
   speech characteristics, 85
   speech intensity, 88–89
    average level, 88
    levels of speech sounds, audiogram, 90
   summary, 93
   vocal sounds following a constanant, 89
Speech audiometry, 38–41
   Kindergarten Phonetically Balanced
     Word Lists, 40–41
   speech discrimination test, 40
   Speech Reception Threshold (*see*
     Speech Reception Threshold)
Speech discrimination test, 40
   Phonetically Balanced Kindergarten
     lists, 40–41
Speech Reception Threshold, 38
Children's Spondee List, 38, 40
definition, 170
Speechreading
  advantages of, 106–107

limitations, 106
philosophy of, 106
predictive considerations, 107
use of, 84, 105–107
visual focus of attention for, 106
Spondee, definition, 170
Staab, W. J., 176
Standard deviation, definition, 170
Stanford Achievement Test-Hearing Impaired
   Norms, 149–154
  comparison mainstreamed – special schools
    scores, graph, 152
  mathematics grade levels, graph, 151
  reading comprehension, graph, 150
Stanford Binet Test of Intelligence, 69
Stapedectomy, definition, 170
Stapes, definition, 170
Static compliance, definition, 170
Static compliance test, 47
Stokee, W. C., 176
Surrogate, definition, 170
Syntax, definition, 81, 170

T

Telephone alerts for hearing-impaired,
   illustrations
  horn alert, 157
  strobe light attached to phone, 160
  strobe light with loud horn alert, 157
  with volume control, 161, 162
Television device for hearing impaired,
   illustration
  decoder, 166
  personal amplifier, 158
  speaker system for hearing aid, 160
Temporal lobe, definition, 170
Threshold, definition, 170
Total communication, definition,
   170
Tracy, Spencer, 176
Trybus, R. J., 175, 176
Tympanic membrane
  definition, 171
  diagram, 16
Tympanometry
  definition, 171
  types of, 47
   illustrations, 45

V

Van Bergeijk, W. A., 176
Van Riper, C., 176
Velum, definition, 171
Vernon, M., 176, 177
Vibro-tactile, definition, 171
Victoreen, J., 177
Vineland Adaptive Behavior Scale, 73
    sample pages, 76–77
Vocabulary, definition, 81
Vowel, definition, 171

W

Walk, S., 177
Wechsler tests
    Wechsler Adult Intelligence Scale
        (WAIC), 69
        illustrations,

Wechsler Intelligence Test
    (WISC–R), 69
    illustrations,
Wechsler Preschool & Primary
    Scale of Intelligence
    (WPPSI), 69
    illustration,
Weiss, K. L., 175
Whatmough, J., 177
Williams, B. R., 177
Wolk, S., 175

Y

Yanick, P., 177

Z

Zemlin, W. R., 177